THINK OR BE EATEN

Also read:

THE DOT CONNECTOR LIBRARY, BOOK 1:

Climategate, The Marijuana Conspiracy, Project Blue Beam…

(2010; 2015, 2ND EDITION)

THE DOT CONNECTOR LIBRARY, BOOK 2:

Consensus Trance

(Mind Control & Human Experiments)

(2015)

THINK OR BE EATEN

Essays

By Angie Riedel

THE DOT CONNECTOR LIBRARY, BOOK 3

Published by Paul Bondarovski

Copyrights of the articles in this book belong to Angie Riedel.

Selected, edited and published by Paul Bondarovski © 2015.
Publisher's website: www.wariscrime.com.

Text and cover design by Paul Bondarovski.

Print edition ISBN 978-1-512255-84-3

Contents

IN MEMORIAM ANGIE RIEDEL —*By Paul Bondarovski*   7

The Butterfly	13
The Choice	17
The Ghosts of Reality	21
The Invisible Realm	27
Think Or Be Eaten	33
Trillionaire	39
Genuine Truth	49
Right and Wrong vs. The Cause	63
So Free and Democratic	71
What I Have Found	75
Beasts Just Wanna Have Fun	85
Mass Media Illusion	103
Politically Correct	111
Broken Angel	119
The Answers	127
The Law	139
On Being Fully Here	153

In Memoriam Angie Riedel
(1956–2013)

This is not just another book in the *Dot Connector Library* series. Many of the articles that you will find here had been written by Angie Riedel exclusively for the *Dot Connector Magazine* that I had been publishing then and of which I hoped to convince Angie to become the chief editor. She never said no, but she wasn't someone to irresponsibly say yes either, without being sure she would find enough time and forces to invest herself in the project full-time. That's the way she lived and worked. And then my own rather serious health problem started, with two full years in the clinics. When it became clear that I won't be able to get back to work for a long period of time, I wrote to Angie asking her to publish all the articles that she wrote for the magazine on her website. They were too good to stay unpublished for so long. By that time, the first book of the present series, *The Climategate...,* had already been published, and I planned Angie's articles for the next book. She was very excited by the book project, she loved books, though never thought of herself as a book author. She was more in the video, audio and graphics, the forms in which she could express herself without anybody's help. She was a natural born helper, but hated to be helped. I think, if she were drowning and saw people passing by, she wouldn't call them to save her, but rather pretend she's just fine and having fun swimming.

When I got back home from clinics, I tried to contact Angie by mail and by phone, but she didn't answer. There was nothing special in it, it already happened to her to just disappear for some days or weeks. It's only months after that I stumbled upon the short "in memoriam" article that I'm reproducing below, supposedly authored by Vyzygoth. I never contacted him before, so it looks like my emails had been filtered out as spam by his mail client; it doesn't matter, though, since I have known what I wanted to know from this short article, which is as follows.

*   *   *

Although we're aware on a suppressed level that our lives could be required of us at any moment, we are apt time and time again to take for granted that there are countless days in our future. And, for most of us, we're correct in that assumption. However, when somebody leaves this Earth sooner than we expected, our assumption is abruptly shattered by the reality of this life's temporality. And realities such as this one are such unwelcome guests. We are saddened and upset by the loss of the person and rudely reminded that our own mortality might be just around the corner.

One day between the last week of April and the first two weeks of May, 2013, Angie Riedel died.

I had a feeling something bad might be afoot as April drew to a close. I had been concerned about Angie's reaction to the estate-mandated directive requiring her to leave the family home, which was necessitated by the earlier passing of her stepfather. The house had to be put up for sale with the proceeds presumably divided among Angie and her two stepbrothers.

Angie didn't care about the money. She only wanted to stay put. But that scenario wasn't an option unless she could pony up the money needed to secure even this modest of homes in fat Silicon Valley. Angie didn't have the money, wouldn't have the money, and knew she had to go.

I kept in touch with her a bit more frequently after she learned of her immutable fate, but only after I had backed off for a short period to give her time to vent, rage, cry and return to normal. When we did communicate again, she admitted she had gone through the whole range of emotions and finally accepted her fate and secured an apartment—more like a townhouse—outside The Valley. She seemed genuinely happy to have found the place and promised to send me some photos of it when she could.

Angie last posted an audio for me no later than April 23. I believe our last telephonic communication was right around that day. After that, I sent her an e-mail or two just to check in and left one message on her machine before May 5—the day a moving company was to relocate her—and asked her to e-mail or call once she got settled in the new place.

By May 13, she still hadn't gotten in touch with me, but I chalked it up to the upset and hassle of unpacking and getting resettled, yet something didn't seem right to me. It wasn't like Angie not to send at least a quick e-mail. In turn, I called information for the area code into which he was to have moved. There was no listing for her, not even the response that her number was unlisted. This didn't strike me as a good thing. I called her old phone number and was surprised to find it was still working. I left a brief but trepidatious message on the answering machine.

The next week, the week of May 20, I called again and was further disturbed to find the machine had been disconnected. I just listened to the constant ringing and knew that my worst fear was about to be confirmed. I immediately called the Sunnyvale police and explained what was occurring and why I was an interested party. They promised to send officers to the address on a welfare check. They told me to call back the next day if I hadn't heard from them later that day.

I called the next day and the SPD watch commander informed me that Angie had been found deceased. He was very considerate, but strapped for details, because she had been found on May 15. He could only tell me that foul play was not an issue. This whole scenario gives rise to many questions, some of which will never be answered, but in an effort to learn something about what had happened, I filed for an informational death certificate from Santa Clara County. I supply the following information for those who cared about Angie:

She was born in Canada, Aug. 11, 1956, to a mother who was a German immigrant and a father of unknown origin who very likely was Russian. She had been married and divorced. She had been suffering from hypertension and cardiovascular disease. The cause of death was a ruptured aortic aneurysm.

Angie, like most people who have this time bomb within them, did not know she had an aneurysm. Unless it's detected in the pursuit of one's other health issues, it seldom makes itself known until a rupture occurs, and then, death is quick. Aneurysms are referred to as "the widowmak-

ers" for their silent and swift disposition. The aneurysms in most people never rupture, but if an event takes place, it's thorough and immediate. Angie's next of kin, a first cousin whom I contacted, was good enough to fill in some details.

Angie was found in bed, head on pillow, covers pulled up. She apparently died in her sleep. There seems to be no answer as to why Angie wasn't found May 5—the date the movers were to show up. The house was found with nothing packed, though the moving service may have been contracted to perform this task as well. The neighbors did not suspect anything unusual, because Angie was reclusive—an adjective that all who dealt with her would find hard to believe. We can conjecture that the emotional upset and the hassles of getting ready to move might have tipped her over. It's possible. But it will never be known. Angie's cousin took possession of her body and had her cremated, her ashes scattered in the Pacific.

Angie was a mystery. She was lightning unwilling to be caught in a bottle. She cycled back and forth between operating a nocturnal and diurnal schedule. If I awoke early in the morning Eastern Time and sent her an e-mail, she was likely to still be awake working on something on either of her websites. Angie was likely a perfectionist, which is a thankless trait, since no one can achieve perfection, but I would say she took pride in everything she touched. She would never slap something together and call it "good enough." At times, when I collaborated with her on a project or asked for something like a graphic to promote a live show I would be doing, she put her all into it. And it showed.

Angie would never ask for money. She did much for many people and never pressed them for a cent. This is why I gave her my archives to sell on her site for her own gain. She told me I need not do that. I told her I knew that, but that I wanted to do this as a way of saying thank you and as a means of compensation for all she had done for me.

In the last year of our association, whenever we worked on something, I would call or e-mail with a verbal concept of what I thought the graphic should look like, and it got to the point where it seemed I only need think it, and she would nail it, but still she would come back with three choices. I'd say something like "Number two. That's it." And she'd laugh, "I knew it. I knew it."

Through that last year, though, it seemed Angie went quiet more frequently and for longer periods of time. That's what it seemed like to me. I would cautiously ask if she were okay and, at times, she hinted that she hadn't been feeling that well, yet she would get through it and return to her old effervescent self. I have no idea if that was foreshadowing. To those of us who knew or felt we knew her, it seems anomalous that someone with such an ebullient internet personality was rather reclusive on the block on which she lived, to the point where her passing wasn't recognized by those who lived around her. But it may be that she saved her best for us.

She was exceptionally passionate about life and the world and the way she believed the world should be. She wasn't wrong in her vision, but the unfortunate thing is that she never saw the world make any kind of turn toward that vision she had and, likely, the world never will. And there are times I talk to her and tell her she might be happy she's missed some of events that have occurred since her passing. She'd probably scold me for not having the kind of hope she possessed in a seeming endless quantity. If you do a search on her name, the hits will lead you to a number of her essays that are posted to this day on a varied array of websites. The girl got around.

Angie Riedel passed peacefully in her sleep. All our hopes are that she awoke to a better world. And, if she's in that place, we know for a fact it's a better place because she's there.

Long may you run, my friend, you will not be forgotten.

*   *   *

The internet is a great thing to communicate, to spread the news, etc., but you cannot trust it as a place for your archives. A single Carrington-like event, similar to that already happened in 1859, would be enough for all the data stored on magnetic support to disappear within seconds as if it never existed. Not much better than that, if you take even a relatively old article on the web, 3 to 5 years old, and check the links in it, you risk to find that many if not all of them are already broken; the web sites are mortal just like their owners. But there are articles, which are too important to just disappear this way. This is why

I have decided to publish the present collection, which is kind of "The best of Angie Riedel," as a printed book. It will also appear in Kindle format, but the purpose is above all to make it available in print. My intention is not commercial, the price will only cover the printing and distribution cost. And it doesn't really matter how many copies will sell—however few, they will exist in this world, and with them, Angie will keep on living.

Paul Bondarovski,
April 2015

The Butterfly

Inside its cramped protective cocoon, a butterfly changes from a rotund, crawling caterpillar into a beautiful, graceful, colorful butterfly. It undergoes this metamorphosis in the dark, all alone, with no one to keep it company or calm its uneasy dreams. It sits there and changes, it lays there and sleeps, it sometimes lies within those warm protective walls and listens to sounds outside its dark enclosed walls—the wind rustling through the leaves of a tree, the barking of a dog, the calls of birds as dawn breaks. It sometimes falls into a deep sleep losing all awareness of its life; and it sometimes comes quickly awake because of a pain it feels as its body undergoes its enormous changes.

Does the butterfly know what is happening to it? It has no apparent guidance or assistance as it transforms its entire being from one thing into another. It only knows it has no choice; that whatever is happening is happening, and that it must be so. It has no sense of time as we know it, no sense of urgency, no sense of worry or fear. It just is.

Then one day it is time. It simply feels that it is time, and so it begins to eat away at its shell. It feels an overpowering need to escape the walls that have suddenly become a prison, confining it, restricting it, keeping it from being able to move its arms and legs. It wants to stretch, desperately. So it patiently, quietly, claws and chews a small hole in its shell, then makes a small tear from that hole, then a larger rent from that tear, opening up an area large enough for it to see the light outside; and when it sees the light outside, it begins to push itself through that opening with all its might.

It takes so much energy, and the butterfly is very hungry and thirsty. It knows it has to free itself to find food and water. It also somehow knows that once it is free it will find those things.

After struggling and tugging and pulling itself through the hole, all of a sudden it is free. Unused to its brand new body and unstable legs it collapses into a disheveled heap and lays there next to its broken cocoon until it can gather its senses and muster its strength. It takes many long minutes, even hours, and those minutes to hours are terribly vulnerable ones. It is without defenses and can not yet fly. Does it even know that it can fly? Does it understand that it has metamorphosed from a caterpillar into a butterfly?

It lays there on the branch, resting, breathing hard. It is all soggy and stiff. It feels a strange heavy weight on its back that compels it to stretch as vigorously and as soon as possible. Weak and wobbly, it begins to push and pull at its soggy heavy wings. It manages to slowly lift and stretch them, first the one and then the other. Gentle waves of oxygen and warm sunshine flow over its body sending shivers of scintillating joyous sensation across the thousands of microscopic feathery scales its wings are made of, rapidly drying them in the breeze and warmth. The butterfly's body is vibrating with invisible music.

Now its legs begin to stiffen, it finds its knees and stands up. Then, with all of its might it shakes out its wings and raises them high, then low, up again and down again, coming to understand what they are and how they feel and how to move them. Does it yet know what they are for?

It begins to flap those wings, each stroke drying them more, fluffing and smoothing them to perfection. Up they sweep, then down they sweep, and what a surprise, what a jubilant, terrifying moment when they scoop up a large bubble of air and lift its whole body high off the branch, and none too gracefully. It lurches this way, then that, and tumbles once head over heels. It will either fully embrace its new being and take control of its new life now, or it will fall to the ground and die.

If it continues to think like a caterpillar, it will reject what it now has, and it will fall to the ground and die. But if it thinks like a butterfly, it will fly.

THE BUTTERFLY

In two more beats of its beautiful new wings the butterfly then easily and magnificently flies away. It will not die, it will live; and it will be here to do what it is here to be and to do. It will drink nectar from blossoms and dance on the wind, it will light down on flowers and taste their perfume. It will be a butterfly and it will love its life.

It is the most natural thing in the world for a butterfly to take to the air and be free. It is the most natural thing in the world for every living thing to be free.

Friday, July 31, 2009.

The Choice

You have just been granted a wish. One wish. Irrevocable. Nontransferable. Unequivocal. Right here, right now, today, this minute, think carefully now, you must make a choice between two things. Think as long as you like, within the ten minutes allotted to you for this purpose, then tell me your answer.

Which would you rather have: *great wealth* or *truth?* Great wealth—or truth. You cannot have both, it is either/or, you have to pick one or the other. Wealth or truth.

Wealth?

Truth?

If you should choose wealth, then you will never have to worry about money again for all the rest of your life. Imagine it. Never again will you hunger or thirst. Never again will you have to feel the unrequited longing, the hurt, the humiliation of not being able to afford whatever you need or want. If you want those new shoes, you may have them, just like that. That new leather coat? It is yours. A whole new wardrobe? You can have it today. You can have a new wardrobe every day, if that's what you want, it will never be a problem.

Never again would you ever have to suffer the hardships and disappointments of not having enough money to make ends meet. You would never again be forced to choose between buying food or buying medicine. Your children will have all of the best of food, clothing, toys, necessities, medical care, education, and travel. Yes, you could travel all you want to, anywhere you like. You can stay in the most beautiful hotels and be waited on hand and foot by smartly uniformed professional hotel staff who will rush to bring you anything you desire.

You don't have to stay in that run down old house of yours with the crooked fence and the squeaky stairs and the cracks in the walls and the tattered insulation, chipping paint; those old appliances, all that dust, that depressing mass-produced suburban view across the street.

You can leave all of that behind. Right now. Today. Instead of that dreary ordinary insufficient lifestyle you can have all of the wealth you need to be free forever from all worries about anything.

What's that? You want to know how much money, exactly? No number is needed, there is no specific sum. You will simply possess great wealth for the rest of your life. You will never run short or run out of money. You will have enough money to live every day, year round, in Las Vegas, if you so desire; staying in the most exclusive, expensive hotel penthouse suites, gambling all day and night; your money will never run out. You will always have enough money to do and to have whatever you want. No material thing, as long as it exists and is available to be had by you, will be beyond your reach. You will be able to afford it, no matter the price. That is how wealthy you would be.

That is the up side. But there is a down side too, as there always is, and this you should consider well before you make your choice. A small price must be paid for the gift of great wealth, for the priceless gift of living free from lack and want and financial worry.

That price is this: in exchange for all of your ample material gain you must give up knowing the truth. You will not be able to tell what is true from what is false, you will not know the difference. You won't be able to know for certain whether or not you are being misled or lied to. You will not get a sense of anyone's intent, should someone want to manipulate you for their own purposes and gain. You'll have no way of sensing tricks or lies, con jobs or sob stories, it will all sound the same as any believable thing sounds.

If you look deep into the eyes of a speaker, be he in the pulpit, wearing a badge or a crown and robes, it will lend you no clues. You will not know if what you hear is truth, if what you read or see is truth, if what you are counseled and told to be truth, is truth.

For all the rest of your life you will not know if any person in your life, in any capacity of your life, is honest or deceitful. You will not be able to sense to a certainty whether someone is sincere, if when they say they love you that they truly love you or only love your money instead. You will not be able to sense to a certainty whether those nearest you are really faithful friends or if instead they are brazen back-stabbers who use you and make you look the fool to all who can see you.

If you're thinking you can outwit the price, think again. You cannot avoid the payment price. You will have no internal truth meter, which is something that you currently possess. Whether or not you use it much is another thing, but used or not, you will have to give it up. It must be forfeit. That is the payment price. Your ability to know truth will no longer function and you will never again be able to tell a truth from an untruth with your natural inborn ability to do so. Your heart will no longer tell you what is true, it will not know what is true.

That is all there is to it. It's really no big thing. And if this tiny inconvenience does not trouble you too dearly—and why should it—then you should be ecstatically happy taking the money. The price is not so great, it's a trifling thing. Truth is cheap after all. Certainly there are other ways for you to procure correct assessments, to validate suspicions; certainly you can find others on whom you can depend to wisely council your decisions, to guide you, to bring you the light you seek, to give you the answers you need. Such can be purchased, advisors and experts of the highest caliber are easily obtainable. It's not at all difficult, it's quite easy. It is standard procedure anyway to purchase the council of others. No one in a position of great wealth seeks their answers from within. How ridiculous. It would be unheard of.

Luxury. Security. Life options. Adventure. Respect. Power. The world is your oyster. But do you find the price too steep? None of the finer things in life come cheap.

Isn't so called truth dependent on who is looking at it? And don't these things all change like the weather? Truth is fleeting, is it not? Truth is hard to find, and it is often inconvenient. It's not all that it's chalked up to be. Not really.

Truth is easily ignored; and it is often irrelevant in the greater scheme of things. Truth is not enough reason to hold back greatness of any kind. At least, it hasn't been so far.

Face it. There isn't much call for truth these days, few are really that interested in it. The truth goes down much easier when you make it up yourself, that's what everyone does anyway. The fact of the matter is that making up your own truths, making truths that suit you, holds so much more potential for happiness and love. Plus who would disagree that lies are much more fun and exciting? Naughty little lies are well known to lead to things that are much more fun and exciting than the ordinary mundane things we're supposed to be content with. But aren't those things, which are considered "forbidden" or "bad," the most scintillating, pleasurable things of all? If it were not so, there wouldn't be so much of it around, would there be?

Truth is really just a bore. Does "truth" even actually exist? Is there such a thing as truth, really? It's too silly to worry about to any great degree, don't you think so? Most everyone thinks so.

So, lucky traveler, master … the clock is ticking. It is time to make your choice. Which do you choose? Wealth or truth? Give me your answer. Choose now between wealth or truth, else miss this once in a paradise, once in a dream, once in a million chance of a lonely little lifetime turning into something totally new. This offer can not be repeated. It will not come around again. So tell me, master, what's it going to be?

Monday, February 22, 2010.

The Ghosts of Reality

The universe seems to be impersonal, it has to be. It doesn't play favorites and is unimpressed with things that captivate our weak mortal minds. Still I'm sure it has magic, there is a great deal we don't know, and even more we're not even remotely aware of or can even conceive of. We need to take our arrogant sciences much less seriously, especially the more they appoint themselves masters of reality. They're just a team of goobers who are as clueless as anybody else, only they do it with such arrogance and solidarity you almost half-believe them. That's dangerous, which is well borne out by history.

When has science and medicine ever not held itself in the highest esteem, paid itself lavishly and demanded obedient worship by law, by force, or by command of the King? And many died for it, and worse. Yet, they would not listen when someone suggested they needed to wash their hands before surgery and they ridiculed the woman who brought it up. "Invisible little things?" they guffawed. "Nonsense!" they proclaimed. That basic scenario has repeated endlessly, and still does, and it always will. They don't know everything. I know, it's a shocker, isn't it? Which speaks to a concept I want to bring up for a quick scratch and sniff.

Proclaiming something is true or false by consensus and without checking the facts does not reality make. Our opinion of any given piece of information is irrelevant regarding it's truth or lack thereof. It simply makes it easier to believe a general consensus when everyone else is being a total dumb-ass, but it still won't make it true. It will not transform an ugly truth into an ugly lie. It will still be a truth, even if nobody wants to believe it.

The first time somebody pointed at me and used the word "conspiracy," it hurt in a weird way. I never saw it that way, because there is no mystery or guessing involved. When you take the time and put in the effort to get more information than what they feed you on the primary broadcast portals, you very quickly become educated, and painfully. You find the same characters, seeped in connected darkness, a brotherhood of corruption and criminality, telling the same sorts of lies, pulling the same ugly tricks, looting and pillaging and arranging deaths. It's a good old boys club of deception and wealth mongering, abuse and power, dirty tricks and behind the scenes motivations.

Granted it's a bit overwhelming at first, and you don't quite know where to begin, but every seeker of knowledge has found that no matter where you start, you'll find the same people, the same components, the same connections, the same tricks, the same tactics, the same lies, the same ignorance, the same evil manipulation of the public. It becomes as recognizable as a set of fingerprints, or as distinct as the taste of lemon. You can't miss it. It's not something you'll mistake for something else, it's just ordinary facts, available in the same accepted broadcast and print media, but always relegated to the back sections in obscurity, and entirely ignored by broadcast media.

The truth is there, it's just that the really horrible truth is bypassed, because it would tend to put too much focus on the evil ones we so wrongly trust, and it might end up with justice being done. And they hate that.

After partaking of the greater truths, one suffers painful pangs of betrayal. It comes from releasing the false beliefs we've been fed all of our lives, and it hurts to let go of pretty things, even if you never really had them. In continuing your research you keep expecting to come to the bottom of the barrel, to find it's ending point, but are soon to discover that it has no end. It is literally bottomless, and there is always much more dirt and filth and lying. The more you dig and the deeper you go, the worse it gets. It's much worse than any of us want to face.

It's infinitely more pleasant to keep locked into the provided fantasy and play the roles we play and pretend there is justice and sanity at the helm. For those who are truly cowards, it's the only way to go. But for those who have a deep and abiding respect and need for the truth, you will be punished for it. It hurts.

You'll have to face a spectrum of things that hurt at a myriad of levels. You'll keep asking why, and you'll want to know how people could do such terrible things and have no regard whatsoever for the irreversible harm they cause others. You'll struggle with all kinds of theories from them not even being human to genetic flaws that deprive them of having a conscience, to finally accepting that they're just filthy dirty evil people who are destroying the world with all their might and having the time of their lives doing it. They never get caught, revealed, tried or punished, in fact they make mind-boggling bundles of wealth every step of the way. And people die left and right and suffer every kind of abuse imaginable, and even some that aren't within the realm of imagination. It's hard to wrap your brain around, and I doubt you ever really do.

Once you pull back the veil of lies and take in the view, you see things very differently. You see all of the patterns and all of the people and can recognize their tactics, their styles, and their involvement in things you'd never have believed could have been planned and carried out against innocent people. You now understand that evil is real and that the struggles of history replay this reality over and again. You realize that somehow all the accumulated wisdom of thousands of years of truth about humanity and people and life has been squeezed off, silenced and not brought forward for the next generation to partake of. Without it we are doomed to repeat the errors of naive trust in the powerful who *always* end up *not* being anyone's friend.

We have forgotten this solid fact and instead have been handed tasty bite-sized pieces of crap that we consume and which fill our heads with visions of heroes in government, heroes in war, heroes in capitalism, and they are painted in glorious colors, which we are taught to esteem and trust and obey unquestioningly. And we do. TV, radio and the press have never made it so easy to make so many people oblivious and stupid and so incredibly easy to lead around by the nose.

Wealth and power is consuming us and it is destroying the world, only now they've taken the gloves off. They've always been at it in the background; we knew about pollution, and we knew about nukes, and we knew about spewing smoke stacks and dead fish and mercury in tuna. But we didn't think to connect the endless reports of corruption and bribery and conspiracy, which is not a nutty fluffy bit of nonsense at all. It's one of the most regularly convicted crimes there are.

Why do so many believe otherwise? In spite of the blatant acts being perpetrated on us before our eyes, few are able to disconnect from the syndrome of trusting those wealthy, powerful liars and see that conspiracy abounds and is par for the corrupted course. How can it be that something so real and so troubling and so horribly unacceptable is not believed to exist?

Parallel dimensions. That's what I'm beginning to believe. I think that when one wakes up and takes on the parallel dimension of reality, they literally move into another realm. In that realm they can see things that regular people cannot. They are at an advantage of perspective and can understand what they see without the restraints of social programming, which, dear friends, is so real that it's not funny. Stepping outside of the bounds of what they want you to see frees you to see what's actually there. It's as obvious as the sky, as obvious as one's own breath. But can you tell the uninitiated about it? Fat chance.

Moving to another dimension allows you to walk side by side with those who are still in the old dimension. You appear to them to be in the same earth plane as they, and they can see you, and you can see them and interact with them in limited ways. However, they cannot hear you unless you speak to them in words and phrases from their own dimension. Attempting to speak from your own dimension causes immediate fear, panic, rage, and a whole bevy of crisis. You scare the crap out of them.

It must be something along the lines of seeing a ghost. An apparition, something from beyond, something that speaks of an undeniable mysterious truth, and this scares people nearly to death. People are much more comfortable with not knowing, with assuming all is well on the other side of the veil, than they are with any facts about it. They don't really want the facts, they just enjoy flirting with the dangerous unknown. It's a rush, it's a scintillation of the senses, it tickles the imagination, but in the end it leaves the world beyond the familiar veil as mysterious and unknowable as always. What they fail to appreciate is that it's a choice, not a sealed door. The beyond is knowable, anyone can step across and know it, but few are willing. As much as they love to flirt with the glittering bits and pieces of ugly truth, they staunchly refute that truths exist beyond what they themselves agree to be real and true.

It's as if majority consensus is all there is to determining truth and reality. It isn't. It just makes it a majority consensus to hold that belief. And hold it they do, with all of their might and without humor or any semblance of open mindedness.

Speaking the truth around those who don't want to hear, it is a supreme waste of time, and fairly dangerous. As if it's not enough to have to endure the personal pain of betrayal and lies you've discovered, you must now also endure the barrage of anger and hatred coming at you from the old dimension, from people who once respected you and now can only think of you as someone who's flung a mental Frisbee and gone off after it into la la land.

It's never based on their effort to come over and show you you're wrong with proof or anything like that, it's always just a pronouncement. We say you are wrong and vile and creepy for saying these things to us, and you are not our friend anymore if you refuse to acknowledge our perfect world and be like we are. Geez, I may love you, but I cannot respect that. That's just obtuse.

I know I'm a ghost in their reality and I get that. It's just such a shame that everything there is to know is rejected outright in favor of staying in a dream, and it's not even that great of a dream. We do love our dreams and we prefer to choose our realities based on what feels good and what's constantly pumped in the mainstream portals, and we prefer to keep everything else at bay. We'll hate it, attack it, vilify it, call it names, accuse it of badness and evil, but, God help us, we'll never check it out. We'll never prove it wrong, we'll never get our hands dirty and crawl in and look for evidence to the contrary. We're so arrogant we believe that anything we think is top notch truth, and whosoever questions it is shot down like a dog in the streets.

If our society is this heavily addicted to fluffy sweet pink lies and phony security based on literally nothing, then what can a ghost do? How can a ghost say, listen to me, when the sound of its voice terrifies the listener to the point of collapse? We ghosts must come to grips with the frustrating truth that where we have gone is not a place for everyone. It takes a brave soul or at the very least a genuine seeker of truth. There are few of either around these days.

It is incredibly difficult not to be able to convince someone to get out of the way of an oncoming train, but you can't physically pick them up and move them, and because you're in a different dimension, you cannot affect their beliefs. They see the oncoming locomotive as an omen of happiness and joy and candy canes and favorite TV shows forever, not as a guarantee of being squished to death and cut into pieces in seconds. If you rage at them and call them stupid, of course, they will react from ego and say terrible things back. They cannot hear us. They choose not to see what is there. A taste for sweet lies is addictive and, like any addiction, is a terrible waste.

Bringers of the truth are reviled by the ones being lied to as well as the ones doing the lying. It's risky business and it wins you few friends. The whole of the truth leagues are accepted to be loony toons and are dismissed, it really does nothing for your career or your relationships to be living in the parallel dimension of becoming self-informed. You lose the dream lie and all of those who exist in it, because they want to stay there and resent your growth and your desire to bring them with you. All you can do is keep offering tidbits now and then, hoping to inspire the curiosity it takes for someone to take it upon themselves to begin digging and finally enter the realm of the next dimension.

But they must come of their own accord, and it's almost always when the big fat ugly truth barges into their own personal lives and poops on them. No one believes it happened, and soon they are shunned and pushed away, labeled nutty, conspiracy theorist, loony toons.

I guess it takes the monster of reality to bite you in the ass before you can no longer deny it's existence, but you will come across alone. I feel your pain. Welcome to reality.

Wednesday, January 24, 2007.

The Invisible Realm

Our bodies are formed from the elements of the Earth, we literally come into physical existence out of the Earth. Where does our consciousness come from?

We know that everything that exists comes from something else that exists. Living things come from other living things, each according to its kind. Consciousness then could only come from consciousness.

Is consciousness created during the process of human reproduction? Is it carried by the sperm to the egg, or does it already reside inside all those eggs? That doesn't make much sense. Nor is there much reason to believe it.

Consciousness is not a physical thing. It has no physical elements to be constructed out of. It has no physical structure. No size or weight or depth or breadth. Our minds and souls and dreams are not physical, but they are real. We all have them, know them and experience them. Their existence cannot be denied, even though they cannot be proven to exist. Nonetheless they do exist.

Does the lack of proving they exist mean that they do not exist? Apparently not. It would seem to mean that things can exist whether we can prove it or not.

Nonphysical things exist in nonphysical form. Consciousness comes from consciousness. Isn't it safe then to say that there is a nonphysical realm of conscious existence? And that consciousness comes from it? It would seem to be so. Why are we so reluctant to believe in the existence of a nonphysical realm? Why do we dismiss as absurd or impossible something that is a lot more likely than not?

The nonphysical realm is something quite different than our physical one. It has no physical form. It's not physical. So where is it? Do nonphysical things need a physical place to exist in? Or do nonphysical things only need a place to exist in a physical realm? If so, when they are not in a physical realm, where are they? Does the idea of "where" even apply to that, which is nonphysical? Maybe a better question is when does "where" apply to nonphysical existence?

Oh, boy, this is getting confusing. Maybe it doesn't make sense to try to apply physical concepts to a nonphysical realm; to things that we know to exist that we can't prove to exist using physical forms of detection or measurement.

We know our consciousness is here with us. It is not separate from us. Is it alive? Our bodies are alive. No part of our bodies are not alive. Everything in our living body is alive. If any part of our body is dead, we are in deep trouble. Unless it is excised, we will sicken and die. Consciousness would have to be alive.

Our physical bodies die and return to the earth. But living consciousness is not physical. How could it die? Where does it go when our bodies die? "Where" does not apply. It does not die. It doesn't go anywhere. It just is.

It comes from is. It goes to is. It just is.

Well, that can keep you up all night thinking about it. It still won't get you anywhere. There is nowhere to get. There is only is. We are in it. It is all around us. You're soaking in it right now.

We can't find the invisible realm, because there is nothing to find. It isn't in a place, it just is.

Are we separate from the realm of living consciousness? Can we be separated from something that has no physical coordinates?

Why do we believe that there is some kind of curtain between us and the nonphysical realm? Is there a veil there? Or is it that our physical bodies cannot enter the realm of the nonphysical? What would prevent our nonphysical minds from entering that realm? Can our minds even be separated from a place that has no physical coordinates? Isn't that realm in the same place as the rest of living consciousness? No place? It just "is"?

Do we believe that there is a curtain of separation between the physical and the spiritual because we have been told to believe there is? We are told over and again that there is a curtain that separates us from the invisible. It is a required belief unless we want to be called nuts.

Some people say that there is a place called "the other side." We go to the other side when we die. Not before. And no one comes back from the other side.

Other people tell us that there is no such thing as "the other side," that this is all there is. That consciousness is a product of the brain, the ordinary output of a machine. Humanity is an aberration, a hiccup, and so is all life. They say that life has no meaning or purpose. There are no invisible realms. Our existence is merely a random cosmic accident that has no inherent value whatsoever.

Those who believe so would easily accept that nothing that happens here matters. It would therefore not matter what we do to others or to the Earth. There are no such things as wrong or right. Life is not sacred, it is more akin to a virus. It is destined to burn itself out and that will be that. It's no surprise that those who preach this belief see no problem with any kind of ghastly genetic experimentation and wouldn't see anything wrong with eliminating most or all of the human species. If nothing has meaning, then nothing matters. Do what you will. What else is there to do?

My own analysis finds that belief much harder to accept as true than the existence of an invisible realm of living consciousness. Far too many people from all walks of life and from all over the world and over thousands of years have given accounts of experiences with an invisible realm. How many of us have had personal experiences of things that cannot be explained according to the supposed rules of the physical world we live in? I have had a few of those experiences myself, and I know without a doubt they were real.

It is far from unusual for people to become aware of inexplicable things because of seeing, hearing, feeling or sensing something that is not a part of the accepted order of physical law. People have had a lot of nonphysical reality experiences and have come back to tell us about them. Near-death experiences are often reports of experiences in a nonphysical realm. Many people have seen ghosts. Many have heard voices from nowhere; have even recorded voices that nobody heard at the time of being recorded. These are not rare or unusual events, they are incredibly common. How many more millions of such unexplained events would it take to begin wondering if there is something there to look at? What actually can justify not looking at them when they are so consistent and voluminous?

Something about this seems strangely suspicious to me. It is not a position of reason to insist there is nothing there. That is a position of unreason. It is a position of reason to study what people are reporting. It would be reasonable to consider some things differently.

The physical world won't provide us with answers to our questions about nonphysical things or tell us what happens to us when we die. Our invisible selves are obviously very real. There is an invisible realm. Do we come from it and go back to it like our physical bodies come from the earth and go back to the earth? Can we go back and forth in the invisible realm at will? Don't we live in it? Can we even be separated from it?

Could it be that we once knew all of this stuff and somehow have forgotten it almost completely? So much so that we don't even know that there is an invisible realm of living consciousness, much less that we have anything to do with it? Have we been made to forget how to live in both realms while we're here? Have we been made to forget how to access the source of living consciousness?

Why do the hierarchies of power and control over our lives insist that there is no truth to notions of invisible realms? No life after death? No spirits? No God? No universe teeming with all manner of life forms all around us? We once could not see the microscopic life forms that teem all over us, around us, and in us, until we got the microscope. But they were there. Why wouldn't there be more things all around us that we aren't able to see? Wouldn't it be more likely than not?

In spite of tens of millions of people whose direct personal experience has shown them that there is without doubt much more to our existence than meets the eye, why the continued insistence that it's only nonsense? When consciousness cannot be proven to exist although we know it does, why is it foolish to already know that there is more than this physical existence? Isn't the foolishness in insisting otherwise?

For whatever reasons we are urged to believe that there is no invisible realm, there clearly is one. Why are we told to not believe what we already know is true? I have a feeling that the answer to that question is far more interesting than we might think. The "unexplained" is not all that unexplainable. What really is unexplainable is the adamant insistence that there is nothing there, when we know there is.

Monday, August 15, 2011.

Think Or Be Eaten

Tonight was a monumental occasion, in a small at-home sort of way because The Tink, who is just reaching nine months old, got his very first collar. It's a stylish little thing, all in black and white zebra stripes. Très chic, as these things go.

I took the bell off as I know no self-respecting cat, no master of stealth and silence, could possibly retain his dignity with a tinkle bell announcing his every stride. And I personally know I would not like a bell hanging around my neck either. Therefore, there shall be no bell.

Even though Tink had never seen a collar before, as I approached him to slip it over his head, he instinctively knew he wanted nothing to do with it. As much as I can appreciate that, there is really no choice in the matter. A big, beautiful healthy boy kitty seen outside without a collar would become instant county meat around here. As it is, all dogs and all cats upon being seen by the League of Pet Nazis are immediately deprived of their reproductive organs. It's non negotiable where I live, and frankly, I find that frightening. The government is wasting no time setting precedents for intruding deeply into our personal lives, always under the guise of a "good cause."

Over the last decade, this zealotry has proven to be beyond efficient and has evolved into a religious-like fervor. For the first time in my life my qualifications as a loving pet owner are constantly challenged, and I have been verbally attacked *everywhere* I've gone to try to find a kitten.

The reasons for this are bizarre and quite worrisome. My desire was to have a cat that had not been violated with deadly vaccinations and that had not already been castrated at the tender age of six weeks. I find both of those things appalling. But more than that, they are not necessary, and even more than that, it is not what I want, and that is the bottom line. I am in the surreal position of needing to defend my personal beliefs, choices and decisions, to twits in medical garb who have no concept of who's the boss.

So my search for The Tink took three years, and I have been repeatedly accused of being a socially deviant animal hater, because I don't believe in butchering baby animals or injecting them with vile, deadly toxins. Go figure.

If this were really America, it would be nobody's business what my personal decisions around my own feline family members' health would be. In every sense of the concept, it's nobody's business but my own. If I am the responsible party, and I am, and if I pay all of the bills, and I do, then I will make all of the decisions and call all of the shots. That's just how it works in the real world. Outside opinions are nothing that should ever be able to obligate me. And while everyone has the right to an opinion, I have the right not to give a damn what it is. It's a beautiful system. I do miss it.

Where once I could find a new kitten in a local pet shop or from a local newspaper ad in one day, it took me literally three years to locate The Tink. I think that's overkill, and I use the word deliberately.

Anyway, back to the topic at hand, Tink's first collar.

After getting down on the floor with him and petting him for a moment, I was able to slip that zebra-striped gizmo up over his chin, then over his face, and finally over his ears, and then let go. At which time he began to walk backwards immediately in the belief he'd somehow walked into something and could simply back out of it. Pretty brilliant, if you ask me, but, in this case, wrong.

I must confess I did laugh my ass off, but only for a minute or two. He *was* pretty hilarious. I've rarely seen a cat move in that manner. Jerking his shoulders around and walking backwards sort of reminded me of Michael Jackson back in the 80s.

It was obvious Tink hated the collar. He really hated it. And as I type these words, he is sitting nearby staring at me with a look on his face I can only describe as incensed. "How dare you," he seems to be saying. "I will not be enslaved." I honestly, and rather deeply, understand what that must feel like.

Some people say life is a hologram, a flat surface with a gajillion identical splinters twinkling in three-dimensional repetition. As above, so below, within you or without you, choose your cliché. But just like I slipped the zebra-striped collar around this freedom-loving creature's neck, an even bigger collar is being slipped around the neck of this entire country. I am experiencing that same feeling of desperately walking backwards, trying to get it off, and, like Tink, am having little in the way of luck. In fact, it's more like a Chinese finger puzzle in that the harder you pull on it, the tighter it's hold becomes.

For those few of us who are really awake (and you can tell who we are, because we haven't slept in years), it is terrifying to watch the government attaching its millions of cast iron collars around the necks of our citizens. They are invisible to the naked eye, but with special glasses like the ones in *They Live*, you would be able to see everyone walking around with dozens and dozens of collars around their necks. It is very surreal to witness this and at the same time listen to people proclaim that they are free and that this is a democracy. If only we had a few thousand boxes of those special glasses to pass around.

Maybe it's just me, but I think people have the right to know that they are being systematically stripped of rights and freedoms by people who have no right to take them. I just think people should know about things like that. I guess I'm funny that way.

It seemed like it would be the perfect ending to present you with a photo of The Tink in his new collar. Unfortunately, he is in no mood to cooperate with me tonight, and who could really blame him.

My hope is that the next time you are presented with an assertion that you are "required" to jump through another government hoop that never existed before, instead of complying without any thought, first think about what it is that someone you don't even know is telling you to comply to. Ask why it's necessary, decide if it even makes sense, and ask yourself if it's really anyone's business or right to intrude into your personal life in the matter at hand.

Also ask yourself if a King or a Queen would be treated in the same manner, and if not, I assure you, something is wrong. For we are all sovereigns in this country, meaning we are the Kings and Queens of our own lives, and nobody exists who has the right to tell us what we can and cannot do; or what we can or cannot be. That is the birthright of any sovereign being, to live our lives without interference or state intrusion.

If we are law abiding citizens, we should never expect to encounter the government in our lives, our Constitution makes that perfectly plain and simple. We are not here for the benefit of government and authorities. It is they who are supposed to be here for our benefit. They work for us. Their job is nothing more than to facilitate our wishes. It is not the other way around.

The bill of rights is not a list of what we get, it is a list of restrictions on the government. Our rights are not given to us by government, and no one has the right to take them away from us. Yet, our own government is taking them away, because, sadly, too many of us don't understand that simple, astoundingly important fact.

Are you obediently jumping through their hoops on command? Why are they intruding into your personal telephone calls, emails, medical history, financial records, and travel plans? Why are they refusing to answer your questions? At what point did our public servants, whom we pay, become our masters?

They have managed to attach their collars to our necks, and now that they have us on leashes, they will yank us wherever they want us to go. Are we willingly becoming slaves of the state? Are our servants calling the shots, and are we then to obey them without question? I wonder how many of us have abdicated our thrones in the belief we will be safer beings; and have done so without even realizing it. We have fallen into the trap of believing our trusted servants, even when they are stealing our property before our eyes, even when we catch them in continual lies, and even when we demand explanations that are met with refusal and the catch-all excuse of state secrecy. The fact of the matter is, no one will ever protect us except ourselves.

A good intention is not the same thing as a good plan; and a stupid sovereign would probably be an almost irresistible mark for a corrupt slave. If we lose our discernment, and if we arm our slaves and allow them to run our lives, the tables will fully turn. The Kings and Queens of America will be reduced to irrelevancy. The bottom line is this: When you no longer have a kingdom you are no longer a king.

Think Or Be Eaten.

Wednesday, December 20, 2006.

*   *   *

P. S. Next day, right after lunch, I stepped into the bathroom to brush my teeth, and as I stood there brushing, something caught my eye.

I turned and glanced down at the doorway. Tink was sitting there like the great Sphinx looking at me with a very strange, wide-eyed, comical expression. It was that, but it was also guilty-looking. It's not unusual for Tink to dog me into the bathroom, but what was unusual was suddenly noticing his brand new collar fully extended on the floor in front of his paws.

He had gotten it off.

The thing is, I did not have the physical ability yesterday to override the safety clasp, which ostensibly should release with a firm tug. I almost pulled my dang brains out and couldn't get it to budge. I'm not a physicist, but clasps aren't rocket science. I'm telling ya, the thing was not going to budge for anyone. I wrote it off to crappy manufacturing, you know—the usual, and forgot about it.

I closed the clasp again and tried to pull it apart. No go. Impossible. No mere mortal could do it.

How did Tinker the Stinker manage to not only get it open, but lay it out in a straight line at my feet? What a funny boy. He *really* wanted it off, and as I see it, if he was so bothered by it that he used kitty scalar technology to overcome it, he should probably get his way on this one. At least for the time being. He is an indoor-only kitty, so I suppose a few more weeks without a collar would be all right. And perhaps a different one should be tried. A scalar-proof collar. I should probably call around first on that one.

This was a great example of wanting your freedom bad enough to overcome someone who thinks they have the right to deny your free will. I couldn't get the thing open, but Tink did. And he doesn't even have opposable thumbs. All of my supposed advantages were not nearly as bodaciously superior as I thought.

The moral of the story? Just because somebody thinks they have the right to run your life, and even though they hold all the cards, it is no guarantee of success and no more true than you tell yourself it is.

And that's all there is to it.

Thursday, December 21, 2006.

Trillionaire

For those who laugh at ideas of conspiracy, it is time to take a walk in the most expensive shoes on earth.

Imagine having personal wealth in the trillions. Wealth you've had all of your life. You've never set foot into a grocery store, you don't even know what one looks like inside. You've never cooked a meal, made a sandwich or washed a single dish. You have servants that buy the finest fresh foods daily, even procuring your favorites from around the world. You have personal world class chefs who cook every meal you eat and servants who serve those meals to you in the appropriate dining rooms: the breakfast nook, the luncheon room, the formal dining room. You've never seen a Chips-Ahoy cookie or a Cheeto, in fact, you've never even heard of them. You don't eat any junk food at all and would be disgusted at the thought.

You've never given a car a tune up, or washed one, or even put gas into one. You have a chauffeur staff that sees to all of your vehicles, and they are always spotlessly clean and in perfect working order. You've never bought a piece of clothing off the rack, or picked up a 3-pack of underwear. Every article of your clothing is made by your personal tailors, including your underwear. You've never gone to the bank, used an ATM, or ever experienced having to wait in a line. You have staff that takes care of all of that for you.

You've never had to wait in a doctor's office, or spend any time in a local hospital. Your doctor visits you, wherever he's from, and wherever you are. If you must have surgery or hospitalization, you'll go to one of the exclusive clinics in Europe, where no working class people are even allowed, even if they could afford to pay for it.

In fact, you've never done anything that most people do every single day of their lives. You've never gone shopping, changed a diaper, scrubbed a toilet, used an iron, or been on a job interview. You've never applied for a credit card; and your credit records aren't even listed by the major credit bureaus, they're private.

You've never once compromised yourself in order to get a paycheck. You don't follow the rules, you make them. You've never had a thought about getting through the month, or wondered how you were going to make your mortgage payment. Your many expensive homes around the world are fully maintained by staff, and are paid for.

You've never had a sick child you couldn't afford to get medical care for, or had to choose between food or medicine. Your children have first class medical care in your own home, and the kinds of pharmaceuticals you use are not available to the public, or even known to them. You are able to maintain optimal health and extend your life with them. You have no fear whatsoever of cancer or most diseases, and you've never taken a vaccination, and would never agree to any. You own all of the pharmaceutical sciences anyway, and the real breakthroughs, the real cures, those you keep for yourself. The masses don't deserve them.

No one ever tells you no. No one. No heads of state, no CEOs, no bank presidents, no generals. No one. No one criticizes you or corrects you. No one dares to show you disrespect, and whenever you speak, you are obeyed. Immediately. With smiles. And you never have to get your own hands dirty, not even once.

Your day revolves around your money. Your money and your power put you in an entirely different, and largely invisible world to the other 99% of people on earth.

All of your "friends" aren't really friends, they're business associates, lawyers, royalty, people with enormous personal wealth, owners of huge multinational conglomerates. There is nothing you can't afford, nothing you can't have, and very few you can't buy. And the ones you can't buy, you can delete, in any number of ways. You have staff that will see to it.

You fear no policeman, no court, and no nation. Your name or face will never be in any newspapers, or in any Google Search. This is easily guaranteed, because you own the world's media. Or most of it. The others are made to comply through various means. No FBI, or CIA, or MI5, or Mossad agents will ever be allowed to so much as sniff in your general direction. They all work for you, whether they know it or not.

You call on Kings and Queens and tell them what to do. You are capable of arranging any form of nightmare for any individual, group, or even nation on the planet without regard to fame or status or human rights. You don't have to care about anything or anyone but yourself.

You believe your wealth makes you superior to others, more intelligent, more deserving of the finest things, justly deserving of the power it bestows on you. You believe it entitles you to run the world however you wish. You don't have to discuss it with anyone, and you never need permission to act. You do what you please.

You, and a small, exclusive group of the most super-rich persons on the planet realized long ago that your mutual goals could be much easier met if you worked together, instead of in cut-throat competition. So you meet annually, and you talk about what direction you want the world to go. You carve up the world's resources in high-powered meetings with a handful of other super-wealthy elites, and agree to an overall global plan. You can start wars and will allow certain underling counterparts to achieve piddling wealth and power, a small reward for their obeisance. You choose the heads of states, and you lay down the real law. They are all under your control, in one way or another. They don't need to know how the power grid is laid out. They only need to know what you decide they need to know.

It is agreed across the board that super-wealthy elites are the only ones entitled to make global decisions. It is your right, probably by birth into long-standing global-class top wealthy families. With that right comes no responsibility to the people of the world. They are useless feeders, and there are too many of them. Their blood, their diseases, their poverty, their excrement, the sheer volume of it sickens you. They are destroying the earth and using up it's resources. They are growing at an exponential rate too, and are overpopulating the planet with inferior dirty, stupid, poor masses who will never accomplish anything in their lives. Only you can do that.

The danger of the masses comes from the traditional difficulty in maintaining total control over them. They refuse to submit to our will and do not accept our right to control them. We know how to control them without their knowing it, and they are controlled by us now as they always have been. Their sheer numbers would become an immediate threat to our continued existence, if they ever realized how we have indeed gained total control over them. We let them talk of equality and freedom, constitutions and rights, to propagandize themselves. None of those things exist. But because they are told they have them, they believe they have them, in spite of the obvious reality that they do not. They don't have the intellectual capacity to see reality.

These stupid followers are no threat to you, at least, not as long as they don't unite against you. That is why you always control the opposition. You install your own opposition leaders and control what they talk about, what they focus on and what they will never get a chance to see. When that's not possible, you destroy it. Arrest protesters, assassinate journalists, replace heads of state that dare to serve their populace instead of you. No matter what they try or what they do manage to discover, you can make sure it never reaches the public. They can be discredited, made miserable, targeted by authority and be imprisoned for life on false charges; that's easily done, and normal procedure. But any who cross certain lines, they will be killed. It sends the right message to others who might want to try it. They never do.

Keeping your identity secret to the general public is half the battle. The other half is the long-perfected system of global propaganda that teaches them to be submissive to wealth and authority, to see it as justified, even enviable. The invention of the television set made the success record of propaganda take an exponential step forward. It has become the most powerful tool of control in the history of the world. And they clamor for it, they want it. They want it every day, and they sit there and take it all in. Nothing has ever existed to make it so easy. We can train them to see the world exactly the way we want them to see it.

The wealthy will be respected. They should be in control of everything—the nations, the corporations, the law. They themselves are above the law. No billionaire will ever do prison time for murder. Do billionaires murder? Every day. But they get special treatment. They may do whatever they like. The masses have been taught to agree. The law applies only to them. They expect to be punished for their wrongdoing, but they know better than to expect the same would apply to you.

It is profoundly simple to bring the masses to your will. They are so irretrievably stupid. Simple-minded, unsophisticated animals, they lack the intellect to see how they are manipulated in every way, even down to how they wear their hair and what clothing they choose. They actually believe they think for themselves. They believe they are making independent choices, when it is you who decides what they will have to choose from. They cannot even think beyond what you supply them to think about. It never occurs to them that choices and options exist beyond your supplied lists. They never think off the menu, and would never ask what's off the menu that might appeal to them more. They don't believe they have the right to think beyond your choices. They are not possessed of your superior mentality, and because they think like sheep and act like stupid followers, they make it easy to lead them everywhere they go.

They fall for every romanticized flag you wave. Go to war for Patriotism, and they go. Go to war because the enemy is evil and coming for you, and they go. No questions, no self-respect. What is Patriotism but a contrivance to get them on board to do your bidding. They are fools, and they deserve to die.

Right now you and your fellow elites are making the final arrangements to achieve global financial domination and hence control of the entire world. America, the only challenge to your goal of rightful planetary domination and control, is coming down. Where laws used to prevent you from using simple force to get what you want, they have been removed. No one is safe in America now, and nothing can be done about it. It is yours, and you are free to move ahead at the time you've chosen. It's absolutely wonderful.

The nagging problem of overpopulation is being dealt with, but not nearly fast enough. Billions of people consuming precious resources and making no contribution whatsoever. They disgust you, and you see them as animals. Their art, their traditions, their cultures are offensive and of no value. They are all irrelevant in the greater scheme of things. None of them matter, and they are making your personal planet unpleasant.

The topic has come up over the years many times, and you are not alone in wishing to get rid of them. Finally, the subject was taken up for official consideration. While some few of the others in the meeting expressed initial discomfort with the idea, it took little to bring them around. It was agreed, 90% of the Earth's population has to go. It must be done. Ten percent are all that is required to perform as laborers and servants, armed guards and soldiers, farmers, chefs and architects, scientists and doctors. There is no need for artists or writers, they have nothing to offer of any value or pertinence.

So far, their foods have been genetically modified to ensure their offspring will be diseased, malformed, and unable to reproduce. Their foods have been transformed into toxic substances that are sickening them by the millions, and they are dying from cancers and dozens of viruses and diseases, all of which were created by your pharmaceutical sciences. Their farmers are nearly eradicated, no memory of natural food production may survive. They are accepting the mass production of packaged chemicals and nutrients as food. Their water is teeming with bacteria, diseases, and organisms, as well as radioactivity. Your own water is safe, you have the means to make it safe. But they do not, nor do they even suspect they are being slowly killed.

Bio-weapons have been perfected and are ready to be released into the world's populations. It must be done in a way that is not obvious. It requires a period of time to use the media for proliferating fear of pandemics, to bring pandemics into the average mind, and to let their precious official experts publicly claim that pandemics are definitely coming. When the public accepts the inevitability of it, they will not question that it suddenly descends on them, killing them by the tens of millions.

Your elite group of the ultra-rich is selling, and very quickly, an entire menu of false flag threats. Global warming, to strip people of dignity and property, terrorism, to enable military control of all populations. Troops in the streets and no electricity or means to power vehicles will keep them obedient, will keep them from attempting to travel. You need them all in one place. The media will proliferate their expectations of all of these things, always in the quickly believed disguise of good causes, and the people will agree to their own enslavement and executions. Their minds must be brought to believe in what they are told. Otherwise they could possibly ask questions, they could figure it out, and they would revolt against us. Sufficiently roused to anger, they could track us all down and murder us. But when we are certain enough of them believe, we will move ahead without fearing the questions of the few.

Indeed, there is no possibility of a natural global pandemic. Western civilization is immune to the diseases of poverty. But we are lowering that immunity in one of our favorite ways, right in front of their stupid faces. They are rushing to take vaccinations, which are filled with viruses, cancers, toxins, and death. Their simple minds cannot grasp they are being lied to by their precious idealized notion of government. Yet, some are catching on because of that vile internet and its vast informational sources. No problem. As growing numbers continue to refuse, we simply made it mandatory by law. *All* will be injected. They all must die.

Nor can anything man does affect the planet; what rubbish. The natural cycle of the sun is bringing the increased temperature and other changes, but blame the people, and they will accept the guilt and pay the price they are told they must. Nor is there any global terrorism, but they believe it, when we tell them over and again they are in danger. They never ask for proof, they just beg us to protect them. It works so easily and so well, it's almost no fun at all.

We are poisoning everything from their clothing to their oxygen and are stirring international fury to justify a global nuclear war. That will finally get rid of them all. But we will survive. We have taken the steps to ensure it. Ourselves and our small percent of servant class persons. We are accustomed to our lifestyles and have no intention of losing it. We are insulted at the thought of sharing it. The masses must go.

A global clearing of the useless eaters will be the greatest gift to mankind. It will protect the environment and preserve the air and water for your future offspring. They deserve to inherit the Earth free of useless eaters and pollution and irrelevancies. Reducing the numbers of unnecessary teeming humanity is the most noble goal that exists. It will save the world. And in the minds of your elite counterparts would make *you* the greatest hero the world has ever known.

The plan now focuses on the United States. America! Accursed symbol of revolt and freedom for the filthy masses! It is time to pay for your transgressions against the real people, the only people, the pure-blooded superior people, the true ruling class! How dare you revolt against us! You committed the cardinal sin, when you stole the land mass that rightfully belongs to us. You who would dare to assume some right to rule yourselves, to obtain wealth, to own property; ptooie! I spit on all of you. You have set an example for the world that must be punished, then wiped from the Earth's memory forever.

How stupid you are to think yourselves capable or even worthy of having the kind of lives that belong only to your superiors. You have been a pain in our sides for decades, but you again proved so easy to subjugate to our desires. Barely one hundred years ago you owned your homes and property, and we could not get to you. You carried guns and shot anyone who dared trespass on your land. How dare you! That right belongs only to our class! You are peasants! Servants!

So we introduced technology, factories, and suburbs. Your media obediently praised the qualities of moving off your lands and buying our products. Even as you made us wealthier than anyone has ever been in all time, we were forcing you to depend on us for your survival. We showed you commercials and movies and stupid magazines, portraying the average man as someone who could live the life of a rich man. We told you that credit was wealth instead of debt, and you bought it! You still run about today desperately seeking the latest and the newest gizmos, and cars, and appliances, trying to portray yourselves as one of us. Fools! You have no wealth at all. You have nothing. You own no land, you don't own your own homes. And now that we have you utterly dependent on us for mere survival, we are taking away your jobs.

We are sending them away! To China and every other place that wants them, just so long as you don't have them anymore. You are becoming once again what you deserve to be, a third world country. We will have stupendous pleasure watching you suffer and die in poverty, wars, and waves of bioengineered viral plagues. It is deeply satisfying to watch you surrender in stupidity to your little madman presidential puppet!

Yes, yes, keep on wailing about the failure of your government to respond to your needs! We love it! Keep knocking on their doors and telling off your elected officials. It is all good. Anything to keep you from seeing what's so obviously going on. Anything to keep you from uniting against us. You are too weak now, too demoralized, too cowardly to do anything but shiver and beg us for protection. It is so sweet, this irony. And long overdue. Good-bye, you dirty little peasants. You will now bear the weight of the punishment of your disobedience to us. No country in the world will survive what's coming next, and the few survivors will never hear of "America," or freedom, or your precious democracy. They will be born into slavery, and they will remain slaves for all time, serving *us,* your masters, with devotion. Even as we tighten the noose around your neck, America, your stupid masses can't see it. You are making our revenge so sweet, and you are proving once and for all, as your final act, that your kind is too stupid to exist. We are right. We are always right. We have always been right, and we will always be right. And now you'll realize that in your last dying gasps. This is our time, we are finally back! May you burn in your imaginary hell for all eternity for your transgressions against us. Good-bye, stupid disobedient America!

Sunday, December 31, 2006.

Genuine Truth

There's a part in the book *1984* that's stuck in my mind and comes up and around regularly like brain cud. It's something I can't swallow, but I can't spit it out either, so round and round it goes in the background.

It's the part where O'Brien holds up four fingers and asks Winston how many fingers he's holding up. Winston says four. O'Brien asks him how many fingers it would be if the Party says it is five. Winston says it would still be four. What else could it be?

Winston is tortured until he says he sees five fingers, but that's not good enough. He is tortured again and drugged until he actually does see five fingers. That's when the torture stops.

That scene perfectly symbolizes the template of all evil. It defies every natural law of humanity and attempts to deny something that cannot be denied. It's not possible to control another sentient being, not in any true sense. All the techniques of torture and mind games and cruelty, the drugs and the sleep deprivation and all of the grotesque and deceitful mind-shattering techniques that evil people engage in, are all phony cheats. They can get people to believe a lie, but it's still a lie. No lie changes to truth, no change ever takes place. Only the destruction of a sovereign entity's mind and body happens. That's nowhere near the same as actually achieving what they really want. They can't get what they really want. It's impossible.

O'Brien then goes on to tell Winston that they are going to purge him of his "insanity," meaning the truth, wipe his brain clean, meaning destroy his mind, and then give him the great gift of loving Big

Brother, really loving him, meaning overwriting reality on his newly broken mind. And when that happens he will finally be sane and whole and right. Then they will kill him.

As if things weren't bad enough for Winston already, anyone with a grain of justice in their soul would think that Winston had given enough now. He'd given everything. Or rather, they'd taken everything there was to take. Why wouldn't that be enough? Why do they have to kill him?

The nature of the supposed crime was that Winston had once existed with thoughts in his head that were true. They were contrary to the Party, which seriously threatened the party, because the party is nothing but a lie. To think a thought that was not a Party thought was the one thing that could never be forgiven, ever. A contrary thought is taken as a murder attempt, because to reveal a lie is to kill it. The Party knows that everyone must believe the lie, because if even one person doesn't believe it, the lie could be revealed and killed.

What the Party wants is impossible. It cannot ever actually happen that different individuals could live different life experiences that would bring them to think only lies, or rather, party thoughts. There is no possibility or probability of that happening naturally. It is contrary to nature, which means it's not optional. It just is. It applies whether it suits anybody or not.

The external and internal truth of every human being is that we are separate and independent from every other human being; experiencing all physical sensation through our own physical senses, thinking our own self-generated thoughts, fully existing in our own self-generated emotions; while synthesizing all that one knows and feels and understands and sees and touches and wonders about and hungers for and dreams of with the never ending turmoil of a teeming world of activity and discovery happening all around us every second of our lives; this is the first truth of existing. That's what being a human being is, it marks the beginning and the end of a life. It announces the legitimate arrival of a new sentient, independently functional human being. Your mind is you, and every part of you is yours by definition. Nothing of what we are can ever belong to or be automatically obligated to anyone else, because no one else had any say over whether or not we exist. We exist.

To not have any of that is to not exist. And to not have it be there by self-genesis is to not exist. We physically exist to function as autonomous, continuously self-creating beings. That is our primary function. Like washing machines wash clothes and can't do much else, we cannot help but do what we're built to do.

The highest crime between people is demanding by force, by law, by deceit, by manipulation, by threat, by imprisonment, by bribery, by withholding information, by telling lies, by ultimatum, by any means of coercion at all, that someone else must relinquish themselves, in essence cease to exist, and instead become a mere extension of someone else's will; carrying someone else's thoughts, ideas, desires, goals and philosophies. That is a crime against nature as well as a crime against the human species. We can offer, we can ask, we can request, but we have no right to demand and no right to force our will on anyone else. We have the right to defend ourselves from someone else's unwanted intrusion or attacks on our persons, but there is no right to wage such attacks or make such intrusions.

We don't seem to appreciate this nearly enough or understand the basic rules of coexistence. We confuse our own desires with a right to satisfy them. There is no such right if it involves or affects anyone else, and they are not allowed to decide whether or not they want to participate. No such right ever existed, and it never will.

What *1984* shows us is how officialdom tries to sanitize their crimes against nature and humanity with claims to impossible authority and impossible rights to propagate official philosophy and condemn all alternative philosophies as evil. The Party turned all truth on its head and made natural rights into illegal things and illegal things into official rights, just like our own government does today and has done for a long time. What the Party was really trying to do to Winston was expunge his unique mind from existence. Big Brother demanded the mass murder of human consciousness.

It's easy to say that's insane, it is insane. It's evil, about as evil as it comes. What's not so easy is understanding why anyone would want this. It makes no sense. It's a contradiction to want everyone else's unique identity extinguished, but still be surrounded by people. It reminds me of Narcissus gazing at his own reflection in the pond. If you want to be the only person on Earth, then why don't you want to be alone? What is it that is so hard for you about other people not being you? What do you feel entitles you to torture and murder them for not being you, when that is not a possibility, much less a crime? What is it that you really want?

People like this have filled volumes with their excuses and lies, which they tell themselves and each other and then all agree it makes perfect sense and justifies their bad behavior. But it doesn't justify anything. There is no excuse or validation for serial killers.

By attempting to use force of any kind to deprive people of their primary function is to demand that they be expunged from existence. More precisely it's a demand to have never existed at all. It's a demand that cannot be met. No one can exist and then never have existed. It doesn't even make sense.

Even more, there is no reason, need or right to demand that anyone cease to exist. To demand that you stop being who you are is to demand that you kill yourself, mentally, physically, or both, so that someone else may feel happy because you are gone. That is not a reasonable demand. It is invalid.

To me that's natural law number one. If you exist, you obviously have the right to exist. Period. Everything else comes after that, not before.

The thing about natural laws is that pretending they don't exist doesn't get you thrown in jail or punished the way breaking a man-made law does. You can't break a natural law. You can try, and we do try, over and over again, but when a law can't be broken, nothing you do will subvert or override it. Natural law can't be pretended away. It can't be changed or affected. You can choose to ignore it, but it will still be there. If you're at all intelligent you can benefit profoundly from the wisdom of natural law, because it teaches instead of imprisons, it expands you instead of diminishing you, it heals you instead of hurting you. Knowing about natural law is like having an anchor so we know where we are in relation to everything else in the universe, but it's also like a piece of string we can pull on to get some light. It's not the same as *"the"* answers, that's something else. Natural laws aren't answers, they're truths. They're starting points, realities, square one. They apply equally to one and all.

Independent sentience is the square one of human existence. It is who we are. It can't be removed from our existence or be given to someone else. It is as hard to share our independent sentience with someone else as it is to share an arm or a leg with someone else. It doesn't work that way. Our independent sentience is what wills our arms into action and our legs to move our bodies across the room. We can't do that for anyone else no matter how much we wish we could, it's just not possible.

We can't feel anyone else's pain other than to empathize with them. We can't see what anyone else is seeing unless they tell us what it is and try to show us and we want to try to see it, but we can never directly see it ourselves through their eyes. We can come to know others, to understand them, to interact with them, even at incredibly intimate levels, but we will always remain separate, individual and unique no matter how close we become.

Interestingly, it has to be that way. We couldn't love anyone if we weren't separate and sentient and self-generating our every thought and feeling. We couldn't experience that other person if we were a single entity. Then we would be one self, one sentience, and there would be no "other" to know or feel anything for. We could not experience self and others if we were all one mind experiencing everything all at once at the same time. We have to be individually sentient in order to see or think or feel or communicate. Our own life has to be a unique, personal experience in order for us to exist at all. The magic all happens when everyone's doing that and we manage to find some way to interact, communicate and express ourselves to each other; and make our lives and our world into something that matters to us.

That's what Big Brother wants to eradicate from not just Winston, but everyone else. Big Brother literally does not want anyone else to exist. It wants to end existence of all but itself in duplicated, repeating, identical form. A clone society of one person. The Party wants to kill sentience and have itself be the only sentience there is. Why that is, I don't know, but that is what it wants. It's not rational. It doesn't make sense. It wants to remake the world into a shrine to itself. I'd call that the definition of insanity.

"I want you to cease to exist so that I may be happy" is a serious disorder of the will.

It's easy to read *1984* and know these Big Brother people were in a raging disease state and see that people who have this disease are also its primary carriers. What might not be so quickly apparent though is that it happens in lesser degrees, and all too commonly today, in the here and now. For some people it is a full-blown disease. For Big Brother and the Party it was more like Ebola. For others it's anywhere from the equivalent of a sneeze to the common cold to the flu. It can even go pandemic, because this disease can be very catchy.

"I want you to cease to exist so that I may be happy" disease, the exact same disease state of *1984,* can and does affect pretty near everybody to some extent or another, at least from time to time; and it affects some folks very seriously, permanently, and forever. We have a lot of names for the multitudinous ways this disease expresses itself, like racism, sexism, corruption, greed, deceit, oppression, domination, imperialism, fascism, modern capitalism, rape, murder, theft, fraud, war, cheating, bullying, manipulation, rudeness, inconsideration, selfishness, cruelty, disrespect, but while the expressions are all quite different, they all spring from the same disease of the will.

There is something interesting I've noticed about this disease. That is its desperate, paranoid, even hysterical need to label itself as the ultimate form of perfect sanity. It must convince others that it is not a disease, not a disorder of the will, but instead it is the pinnacle of truth and perfected human thought. That assertion cannot be proven, but to the infected, proof is irrelevant. Reality is irrelevant. Nothing is relevant but what the infected person thinks or feels. They can and do make it up as they go. They have no fear of being hypocrites or liars, and they cannot be shamed. They are able to stand before anyone in a state of raging disease, while it is crystal clear to onlookers that they are covered with crawling disease organisms that are truly disgusting and horrible, and they will say they are beautiful and healthy and that anyone who doesn't think so is stupid, or a terrorist, or is insane. They will say all kinds of things about others, but they will never consider any reason exists to look in the mirror.

Even more interesting is that those who are not infected see the disease and its false claims for what they are, and they cannot be tricked, fooled or in any wise convinced to believe it is anything but a disease. They recognize infected persons and know they are infected. It is only those who become infected who will suddenly believe they have not become sick, but they are now perfectly healthy. They too will spontaneously develop the identical paranoid to hysterical obsessive need to be perceived as perfect in their sanity. The slightest suggestion that they are not thinking clearly, that they are not objective, that they are wrong, that they are behaving badly, will never be received objectively or passively. On the contrary, it is risky to challenge infected persons, because doing so cuts to the core of the disease and threatens to expose it, which would prove it is there. Proving it is there is to render it impotent. Knowing it is there is to threaten its existence. The response is predictable and always the same—rage.

The germs of "I want you to cease to exist so that I may be happy" disease float freely about us in great quantity at all times, just like so many other kinds of germs and pathogens. Our mental immune systems are not always geared up enough to fight off bouts of infection from this soul pathogen.

The cure is not complicated, it just takes conscious effort and the desire to get well, or if we are already well, to stay that way. No one is ever immune from being infected by this stuff. Interestingly, though, because it is a malfunction of our own will, we can always choose to not be infected. As soon as we realize we have it, we can choose to not have it.

Being uncomplicated is not the same as being easy. It can be really hard to be honest enough and unselfish enough and mature enough to admit when and under what circumstances we have this disorder. It's not hard to understand that everyday people get infected with this, because it comes from a natural and perfectly good thing. It's just that the perfectly natural good thing has malfunctioned.

My earlier quick definition of a person was that it is an independent sentient being driven by self-interest. It has to be in order to survive. But it also has to be driven by interest in others, because when it isn't, it malfunctions. It attempts to operate in opposition to reality. The reason it has to be driven by interest in others is because there are others. We exist and others exist. Any suggestions of greater or lesser right or worth or anything else are hot air. They can't be supported by natural law. We all exist in exactly the same degree, we have to acknowledge each other's existence in exactly the same degree. If there were no others, it wouldn't matter, but then we wouldn't exist either, so the point is obvious. You just can't get around this, it's simple common sense.

As simple as it is to understand, it's possibly one of the hardest things to manifest. Sometimes it can't be helped just due to sheer numbers, but many times it's only a choice we make to either acknowledge the existence of others or decide that their existence doesn't count as much as getting what we want. When we negate the existence of others by conscious intent, with malice, with depraved indifference, it disrupts and damages the natural order of things and creates havoc, destruction and suffering.

Infected people are the cause of almost every wrong that people do in this world. It's not the same as making a mistake; anyone can make a mistake. This is specifically about the will of the infected individual malfunctioning. And like any systemic disease, it doesn't just affect the will, it spreads to other components of the being and invades them, thus transforming them into willing accomplices, which will aid and abet the disease's continued existence. No disease can go on existing unless it propagates, and this disease is desperate to propagate itself. It must infect reason, logic, compassion, critical thinking, and most every function of the individual being.

The nature of this disease is to demand that natural law does not exist or that somehow it is wrong and they are right. Just as infected people insist they are not infected, but are healthy, the disease can only stay alive by turning everything inside out and calling it normal. This disease exists in direct opposition to simple truth and plain old ordinary reality. The problem is, it cannot affect simple truth and plain old ordinary reality. Because of that it can only try to destroy them. It obsesses over destroying them. It goes on crusades to destroy them. Infected people's only recourse is to use force to eradicate simple truth and ordinary reality, because the exercise of one person's will cannot affect change in any other person but one's own self. Even this unchangeable natural law is one they deny and attempt to overthrow even though it is pointless.

Wanting to use our personal will to control the thoughts and actions of another person is common enough, but apparently not quite common enough for anybody who does it to recognize it doesn't work that way. Our will is confined to controlling *only* our own selves, both physically and mentally. We cannot simply "will" another to do or be what we want. If we could do that, we would do that, but it's not possible.

What does that mean? It's too simple to believe it needs to be said out loud, but here goes. It means that it's wrong to do that. "Wrong," meaning it is not within the realm of possibility. We do not possess the ability, and therefore we do not possess the right, to have our will control the thoughts, beliefs, feelings or life of another person. Those are things we can control and are supposed to control in and for ourselves. We do it for ourselves, others do it for themselves. That's how this whole human existence thing works. That's how we function. Our will cannot affect the basic existence or function of any other being. You just can't do it.

Unless, of course, you do terrible things that hurt other people. You can use your will to make you get a grip and behave like a decent human being, or you can decide not to do that and use your will to come up with ways to use force or deception to make others do what you want. No matter what your supposed good reasons are, no matter how it is rationalized, it is still breaking the first basic rule of coexistence to do that. Just because you are able to use your own will to ignore and defy simple reality and truth does not mean you are right to do so. You are committing a crime against independent sentience when you use force or other cheats to get your way.

You're also causing damage to the person you use force against, and possibly to other people connected to them as well as yourself. There is physical rape, and we all know that's a crime, but there is also mental rape, and that's also a crime. Both physical murder and mental murder are crimes. In a way this is so simple that it's hard. What's hard about it is really facing it, really getting it, and really understanding that we're not functioning right in this world unless we're trying hard to overcome those things in ourselves that make us want to deny the obvious and act as if our desires matter more than who we use to satiate them. There is no natural law to support that.

I know that some will say that's not true, because, for instance, in order to eat we have to kill something. They will say that because that's true, then anything we want to do toward fulfilling our desires is valid, and there are no rules, and killing isn't even wrong. That would be incorrect. That's like saying, "If this is an apple, then everything is an apple." No, it isn't. There is an obvious natural law that requires us to eat life to stay alive. We have no choice but to consume other living things, which means killing them, but those living things are food, not other people. We have to eat food, but we do not have to rape or kill or lie. That's just stupid. Look for the natural law. If it's not there, it isn't there, so quit being a twit. This is simple stuff. It is common sense. You don't even need to be able to read to know this. We can observe it all around us in our natural world.

There are rules. There is right and wrong. We are not masters of the universe. We are complex, diverse, sentient, individual beings living finite life spans on a world with other sentient beings and many other life forms. We're all here together. We like to pretend we're not a part of it all, but we are. The more effort, time and energy we put into pretending we are separate from our shared Earth reality, the more we prove ourselves wrong. The more we try to defy the natural, common sense rules that cannot be changed, the more harm we do. And, boy, are we stubborn and defiant? We hate not having everything our way. It should be pretty clear to everybody by now that we are guaranteed to kill ourselves as we continue killing the world we're a part of unless we knock it off.

Our personal desires may be strong, but they do not automatically manifest a right to be fulfilled. A desire to be fulfilled is not a right to be fulfilled. Our rights end at the outer edges of our own skin. That's the fact of the matter, and it's a fact we sometimes really hate. We can hate it all we want, but that won't change a single thing. We are doing it wrong when we pretend there are no rules and there is no morality and there is no right or wrong. Of course, there is.

The disease state of *1984* is in full bloom in the real world we all live in. Just like in the story, the infected Party power players have lied, cheated, stole, murdered, and turned reality on its ear in the useless attempt to legitimize their disease. They achieved the means to have it written down on paper and have their crimes protected by legal force from any attempts at correction, but they did not achieve the real goal they wanted of making it legitimate. It can never be legitimate, it is a disease state. The next step was to elevate the lie to a sacred truth that must never be questioned or doubted. This makes anyone who questions or doubts it a vile horrific enemy that they can then claim the right to brutalize, imprison, and even kill in "self-defense." It is absolutely self-defense. Every person with the truth inside them is a direct threat to their continued existence.

When the disease state controls our lives, everything slowly dies, because the disease brings death. That's what diseases do. Natural law facilitates life and growth and health, because that's what it does.

I know *1984* is a book of fiction, but all the same I would beg to differ. It's a fictional account of hard reality and it describes perfectly well the nature of the eternal struggle on this world. It shows us the exact definition of "wrong." It shows us how "wrong" masquerades itself as "right." It shows us how to get people to never look at the real issue and instead believe the wrong people masquerading as right people, and to embrace the masquerade wholeheartedly and think it is real. It shows us exactly why information control and non-diversity of thought turns people into automatons who don't think and who cannot think past their indoctrination. It faithfully depicts what happens to people when their birthright to think for themselves and to have their own opinions, beliefs and ideas is cheated and manipulated away from them.

As unpleasant as these things are to look at, they must be looked at. They must be endured long enough to make clear to us how important it is to know with all certainty what is right and what is wrong and why. Because as long as we fall for the rivers of bullshit and lies that are there to detour us from simple truth, to confuse issues that are not confusing, to excuse behavior that is inexcusable, we will continue to slowly but surely cease to exist. And if there is anything the vast majority of humanity would be quick to agree with, it is the fact that no one's demands that we cease to exist can ever be legitimate. We are never obligated to cease to exist to make anyone else happy.

That means that the very people who are most infected must also be allowed to exist. But at least once we know who and what they are, and if we care about being free of their infection in ourselves, we can choose any number of legitimate avenues to address this disease and perhaps even some day be able to free ourselves from the rampage of death and destruction it inflicts on our whole world.

We are given to believe that things are much more complicated than this, that nothing can be this straightforward and simple and be real, and that it would be idiotic to suggest that there aren't puffed-up self-important people who are better than everyone else based on any number of personal beliefs. But a personal belief is not a genuine truth or a natural law. A genuine truth applies to one and all. It applies whether we know about it or not. It applies whether we deny it or not. It is not a matter of assertion or belief. It just is.

An example of a personal truth is that you are afraid of bees. The reason you are afraid of bees is that you are highly allergic to bee stings. If a bee stings you, you are very likely to die. This is a personal truth that is actually a truth. It is true whether or not anyone else out of the next hundred people is also allergic to bee stings. Even if nobody else is, you still are. That's a personal truth, not a general one, or what I refer to as a genuine truth that applies to all people everywhere.

Another example of a personal truth is that your mama says you're special, and you believe her. She would never lie to you and tells you you're special every single day. You might really believe you're special and your mama might really believe it too, with all of her heart. But it doesn't make you special anywhere else beyond you and your mama. It's not a general truth, and I'm not even sure it's a personal one, but in any case, it is certainly not supported by natural law. I'm surprised how many people don't realize that. It boggles the mind.

GENUINE TRUTH

The same applies to the personal belief that you are better than others, or more special than others, or more entitled than others, due to whatever variable you want to assert. Your personal religious beliefs, a belief that money determines the value of a life, a belief that might makes right, that real men must be macho and should beat up women, these are personal beliefs, not general truths. They may be true to you, but that does not equate to being true anywhere else outside of your own head, even if you can get fifty-seven other people who say they agree with you and believe the same thing. It still doesn't make it a general across-the-board reality. It is not a genuine truth. It does not apply to all. You can think it does, but it doesn't, and it never will. It's not possible. If it was a general truth, everyone would know it, wouldn't they? But too many people know it's not a truth in their own lives. A personal truth may or may not be true, and it may or may not be a genuine truth. These things are all different, and not all supposed truths are true.

The truths that I'm talking about here are genuine truths. They do apply to everyone across the board. They are something we're all born with in exact equal measure. They just are.

Where we run into trouble time and again is in believing our own personal truths, beliefs, opinions, preferences and desires apply to anyone outside ourselves, which they can't, and don't, and possibly never will, because they're personal. We may think they can apply to others who aren't interested or who reject them, but they don't, and they won't, and they can't. We have to get over ourselves and quit pretending that what we have in our heads, no matter how much we believe it, is not an automatic general truth that applies across the board just because we think so.

We also have to accept that not every desire comes with a right to have it fulfilled, especially not if fulfilling it includes anyone else but ourselves. There is no right to get our jollies out on somebody else's life. This is not so hard. Like I said, the hardest thing about it is making ourselves be honest about it, and for some people that's just too much to ask.

We can't make anyone else be honest or real about anything, we can only do that for ourselves. But we can tell who cares about being honest, who cares about the other people on the planet with them, and who consistently doesn't. We can choose to refuse to associate with people who want to be infected, we can try to present them with other knowledge and facts and ideas to explain how we see things differently, or we can choose to do something else. That's the free will part of being an independently sentient person; and the self same part that the diseased among us are always so desperate to stamp out. What a coincidence.

Regardless of anyone else's take on the subject, this is my take, and I duly register it along with the statement that these are my rules, and if you break them you're wrong. Also for the record is the fact that this is only a part of this picture, there's a lot more attached to it and behind it and supporting it, but it is still a genuine truth that stands on its own. It's still true whether we're able to appreciate it and make headway with it or not. If we don't know this, we won't get anywhere as human beings, but I think a lot of us know this, even if we've never thought it through or put it into so many words. It only makes sense. It's fair. It's reasonable, logical and hard to argue with. It's hard to come up with any genuine truths to support the opposite.

Unfortunately, what we know from *1984* as well as our own current reality is that the truth does not keep some people from trying to pretend their own truth is better or matters more. It does not keep anyone from denying it or violating it or trying to erase it. Which is why it is so important to be adamant about what we know is right and wrong and not allow ourselves to be hijacked out of our very purpose and reason for being alive. If we don't value our independent sentience enough to protect it and insist upon others' respecting it, nobody else is going to do that for us. Indeed, if we don't care enough about it, it will be hijacked and we will be expunged from sentient existence and we will become nothing more than animated meat puppets trained to respond on command as extensions to somebody else's will. That would never work for me, but then I am aware of the rules, so it's much less likely to happen to me. But those who are not aware of the rules would not even know if and when it's happened to them. And that is something that scares me even more than *1984*.

Sunday, June 28, 2009.

Right and Wrong vs. The Cause

There's a lot of head-butting out there these days, something I don't have much taste or tolerance for. I don't see brute force as a proper determinant of winners and losers. Brute force is, in truth, an ultimate position of weakness. Brute force is desperate and afraid of truth. It hates and dismisses truth. It punishes truth. Brute force specifically aims to destroy the existence of truth.

No legitimate thing is harmed by the truth about it. It is only the illegitimate that cannot withstand its own truth being revealed. The truth destroys the lies. Positions based on lies are decimated instantly once the truth about them is known.

This is why it's always been so obvious to me that things like gag orders slapped on whistleblowers, press censorship, police brutality against peaceful dissent and back room political deals are based on lies and reasons that cannot withstand the light of day. Governments that oppress, threaten and violate their own people are openly admitting that who and what they are, who and what they serve, have nothing to do with legitimate leadership concerned with the good of the people they ostensibly exist to serve. Oppressive regimes serve only themselves, and they demand that all people serve them instead of it being the other way around.

Why should the public serve authority? There is no reason for people to forfeit their own needs, wants, beliefs and values to instead serve the selfish self-interests of so-called authorities. Yet, this is the status quo all over the world. But why do the vast majority of people in this world accept and support this arrangement? What do we see happen when authority becomes destructive, oppressive and unjust? That destructive, self-serving authority lashes out with brute force, sometimes killing millions of its own people. Authority would be much more amenable to straightening up and flying right if it did not have the option of using brute force to terrify and destroy its critics. Brute force is weakness and fear personified.

Authorities are mere mortals like everyone else. They have no special qualities that separate them from those they dictate to. People in positions of authority cannot fly or turn invisible or walk through walls or escape death. They must eat and sleep and drink and feel pain and confront the same private challenges that every person in the world must confront and deal with in the course of a lifetime. Authority figures are every bit as prone to weakness and selfishness, dishonesty, deceit, lying, stealing and cheating as the rest of humanity, if not more so, they are not above any of it. They are not exempt from bad behavior. They are not always honest or right or even all that well-informed or well-intended. And the more authoritarian they are, the less likely it is that they'll even really give a damn about the effects their demands have on anyone else.

This is anathema to justice. It is the opposite of what is fair and decent and moral and ethical; in a nutshell, it is wrong. It is purely self-serving. When that self-service reaches the heights of arrogance and cruelty, the truth of who and what selfish authority is cannot be covered up. It virtually screams its true identity and purpose from every hilltop and rooftop.

It is like Godzilla rising up out of the ocean and coming ashore, stepping on villages and power lines and howling as sparks fly beneath its feet. It is not at all subtle. It demands everyone's immediate and total attention. And everything that everyone does can only be in response to this monster on the loose in their lives.

This is nothing new. How many centuries have gone by with this kind of corrupt, self-serving power at the helm of nations and cities and religions and economies, enslaving people and waging wars to conquer and claim the territories, wealth and resources of others? Pick up the newspapers today and read of examples around the world of repressive, violent regimes engaging in slaughter, in vote rigging, in threatening, imprisoning, torturing and killing of political dissenters and competitors. Even here, in the good old USA, we witness republican factions working very hard to remove millions of people from registered voters lists; in particular, people who are poor and black and very likely to be voting for democrats. Republicans are eternally obsessed with finding reasons to call for people's right to vote to be taken away from them. In some states, anyone who has ever been convicted of a felony has had their right to vote taken from them, although this makes no sense and is irrelevant to voting. No one's legal, or moral, or birth rights are ever subject to denial by anyone else for any reason. It's just stupid to pretend it's anyone's call to decide who has rights and who doesn't, and yet we hear this all the time.

Prominent democrats in our hallowed halls of government shamelessly proclaim that anyone accused of being a terrorist—just accused mind you, not proven to be a terrorist—that such persons upon accusation should not be entitled to legal rights, no day in court, no lawyers, no phone calls, not even a basic level of humane treatment. They deserve nothing, once accused, meaning they only deserve to die. This sort of arbitrary condemnation of others is heinous and baseless, and if nothing else, none of our dearly elected, or anyone else for that matter, has any right or business deciding who is good enough to live or die, or who is good enough to deserve equal treatment under the law. But go tell them that, and you'll get a choir of Sarah Palins in your face.

When it is so clear that people who behave this way are illegitimate at the very least, and it is obvious that this self-serving, judgmental, repressive arrogance and hypocrisy is destructive to the people, then how can it be so pervasive and growing stronger by the day? Why don't people see it for what it is? How can filthy lying whores like Rush Limbaugh, Fox News, most of our dearly elected and the far-right political/ religious extremists be able to capture and recruit so many Americans and bring them into their demented, destructive fold?

What it boils down to can best be summed up in a question. Which of these two things do you believe is the most important?

1) Knowing right from wrong,
   or
2) Supporting "The Cause"?

Because it is the clash of these two immovable forces that causes the outrage, resentment, fear, intolerance and outright hatred battering our country into bits and pieces of security-obsessed, unconstitutional, inhumane, disastrous self-destructive cluelessness.

It very much matters which one you pick. Let's look closer at those choices and see why.

Right and Wrong

For different people to live peacefully side by side, they must have just one important thing in common. They must agree to the definition of right and wrong and then abide by that definition. As long as all parties involved do that, not much else has to be held in common.

Right and wrong are impartial. They are no respecters of persons. They see no rank or status or wealth or philosophy or religion or political affiliation. Right and wrong are right and wrong, no matter who you are or who you think you are. Right and wrong are the same for everyone. If it is wrong for you to kill, then it is also wrong for me to kill. This is simple stuff, a child can easily understand it. Regardless of choice of or lack of religion, right and wrong still apply the same across the board. Regardless of nationality, gender, age, income level, education or lack thereof, right and wrong apply the same to one and all, and can be understood by one and all.

Supporting The Cause

Enter "The Cause." The greater good. The war effort. The church. The political party. While we're at it, toss in the ugly underbelly of human weakness: racism, sexism, religious bigotry and all bigotry including heart-swelling nationalistic love of country. Conflate heart-swelling love of God with heart-swelling love of country, and you've got the mother of all righteous causes to support. Suggesting otherwise would likely get your ass kicked, at the very least.

Ever since that horrible moment when g. w. bush looked the world in the eye and said, "You're either with us or you're against us", he set in motion the exact recipe for disaster that would culminate in the ultimate destruction of America. He probably didn't set out to destroy America, but he certainly did achieve exactly that. Why? Because his entire premise and foundation was an untruth. He was just plain wrong. There are many more options than either being with us or against us. Asserting there are no other options sealed America's fate. The entire foundation of his war effort, his war on terror, the national security state, his beliefs about market fundamentalism, all of it, was wrong. Wrong in the sense of right and wrong. So, in essence, what sounded like righteousness was a hollow foundation, a foundation that could not exist and never did exist. All the cheerleading and belief in the world would not turn empty air to wood or stone. There was no "there" there. There is still no "there" there. And all of the lying, scrambling of facts and figures, obscuring of information, secrecy and congressional bills passed in the world cannot change that. It is all based on a lie compounded by hundreds and hundreds more lies to try to cover and support the first foundational lie. To use a word I've grown to loathe, it's simply not sustainable.

Supporting The Cause supersedes right and wrong, and that, of course, is untenable and false. You cannot ignore and defy right and wrong any more than you can ignore and defy gravity. You can try, and they sure do try, but you cannot succeed. Supporting The Cause by definition includes doing whatever it takes to prevail. That specifically means ignoring right and wrong. It specifically means becoming monsters "if need be," in order to assure that our cause emerges victorious. When nothing matters but supporting the cause, then all actions proceed from extremes of selfishness. By contrast, when right and wrong decides our behavior, we are thinking of others, and not only of ourselves.

Supporting The Cause means looking the other way when you see horrific wrongdoing, corruption, murder, any and every wrong thing. Because The Cause is all good, then to criticize it is to say that it is not all good. To say that it is not all good is to be against it. It makes you a threat to The Cause, it makes you the enemy. It must be "My country right or wrong," no matter how wrong it gets. It will be "My religion is good, your religion is not my religion, so it can only be bad. You are not on my side, so you must be my enemy." This is thinking inside "The Cause."

Supporting The Cause has created euphemisms like "collateral damage" to describe and excuse the deaths of innocent civilians. That's just one example, but there is a virtual library of such euphemisms. Supporting The Cause has enabled and funded the existence of covert departments of government that overthrow governments in foreign countries, so much so that it would be foolish to believe it hasn't been happening here as well. Of course it has been. To those who do this work it is all for a greater cause.

The Cause is completely egocentric. It becomes the only thing that matters. It doesn't matter how many people die or how much injustice is wrought, all that matters is supporting The Cause. The Cause can only see The Cause and nothing else. People are used for the good of The Cause. Murder, torture, false imprisonment, cruelty and abuse go hand in hand with supporting The Cause. Because The Cause supposedly defines and stands for the highest definition of what is right and true and good, then it would only seem logical that nothing done for the good of The Cause could be wrong.

But that would be wrong.

Causes are transient and fleeting. Right and wrong will still be here after The Cause blazes through and torches everything to ashes. Right and wrong are irreplaceably valuable. Right and wrong guide us. When right and wrong no longer matter, then what is left? Arbitrary brute force to achieve whatever your selfish aims are. And that is precisely what America has devolved to. It now approaches every threat, real or imagined, every challenge, every problem, every annoyance, every failure to fully submit to its will with overwhelming force. It throws hundreds of billions of dollars at military might and security forces, equipment and training, and everything else has been thrown under the bus, including the people of this country along with their well-being and future. Now the people are the suspicious enemy. The people are being scrutinized to determine their individual allegiance to "The Cause." Those who don't care about false causes or meaningless labels and instead put human life and simple right and wrong first, they are becoming the enemy, the new domestic terrorists.

There is nothing wrong with loving your country, or loving your God, or laying down your life in support of what you love and believe in with all of your heart. What is wrong is believing that the most private and personal choices people make in a free world, like who and what they love and believe in, has to be the exact choices you make, or else they are your enemy. That is wrong. All any of us have a rightful expectation of is being treated the same as others inside a community that knows the difference between right and wrong and otherwise leaves us alone.

The Cause can never leave others alone, because it is desperate to prevail. It exists only to prevail and for no other reason. It is forever asked to prove it is right, but it cannot. All it can do is try to kill dissent, literally, until everyone is dead but those who support The Cause. And if that is not the very definition of evil, then I don't know what is.

Monday, January 3, 2011.

So Free and Democratic

A long, long time ago, before there were such things as politicians, people used to talk to each other and tell the truth. They simply spoke their thoughts and feelings and talked of their experiences and pondered life's questions, sorrows and joys openly. They had nothing to hide and no reason to connive or contrive for people who were more than likely relatives anyway.

You'll have to check me on this, but I suspect that right after someone invented money the first politicians showed up, about five minutes later; and sadly, it seems politicians will never go away. As long as there is money flowing freely out of the people's pockets and into the taxman's coffers, there will be politicians.

And as long as there are politicians, they will do what politicians do, which is to loyally serve their only two real clients, the rich man and the tyrant, both of whom forever want only one thing: *everything.* They want more than anyone else, more than anyone needs, more than even makes sense. They want control over what is not theirs, because they want what is not theirs. They require special rules, which exempt them from legal, moral and ethical behavior in order to get their hands on what is not theirs.

They also want other rules, which will literally or figuratively disembowel anyone attempting to protect what belongs to them in order to keep it from being taken by the rich man and the tyrant. They want many special rules like exemptions from paying taxes, exemptions from legal responsibility for their harmful acts against others, and special legal privileges that allow them to pay cash to the state in lieu of life imprisonment or public hangings for felonious acts as would befit any other citizen. The politician's job is to facilitate their clients' receipt of these things.

The steps of facilitation are simple and straightforward. It is done by accepting generous amounts of money from their clients to purchase one or more performances, the standard political play-acting of saintly state's rhetoric delivered with bellowing voice and masterful language, complete with fist pounding debate, name-calling, character assassination, bribery, blackmail, and so much more. Every trick and tool in the dirty little politician's toolbox will be used behind the politician's back, while the front side delivers windswept drama dripping honey-thick oration toward winning the objects of their dear and generous clients' hearts.

All of these things are done while the politician publicly pronounces himself to be the trusted friend of the people, a friend wholly devoted to whatever they want to hear, a literal physical embodiment of lily-white virtue and honor, a valiant protector of all that is righteous, noble and true; and most of all selfless. Politicians must scratch and claw their way to the tops of rarefied marble pedestals, where they then are able to pronounce their selfless saintliness and honor to all the good citizens of the state, rich and poor alike. This is the first lie of politicians.

But it is hardly the last. When one's first foot forward is a balls out, shameless and preposterous packet of lies, then nothing else can follow but more lies. Indeed, one must lie from that day forward about every single thing. As years go by, the depth, breadth and sheer number of lies, deceits and manipulations stack up into inextricably interconnected layers built up into great kingdoms made of stale, bug-infested crackers. It is nothing but a house of cards, having no substance, no glowing record of good deeds done, no evidence of the people's quality of life having improved, no trace of selflessness or all that much service.

There will be a great deal done that delivered generous portions of self-enrichment, but these are never shared with the public, they are taken home and used to enjoy a much better quality of life than the average citizen could ever dream about. After achieving such a dubious track record, any grandiose proclamations of service and nobility are transparent enough to expose the facade of a crumbling cracker kingdom and to make clear the complete lack of shining alabaster castles and towers.

The jig should be up, but the other politicians will now expound upon the noble and glorious career of their fellow public servant until he dies, and then afterward too, because it is in their best interests to continue pushing the first lie of all politicians.

The people are always told that politicians are decent people with no personal agendas, qualified people, people who do not lie, cheat or steal, who love their country, love their people, worship the same God the public does, and work long, hard hours battling out legal concepts in order to ensure prosperity, freedom and democracy for all.

They have to say things like that, because if they told you what they were really doing, they'd be tarred and feathered and run out of town or hung in the public stocks for weeks to let children laugh at them and throw rotten produce at them, and then they'd be executed for being the scum of the earth.

Because, in a nutshell, politics is a series of agreements made between the rich man and the state wherein the state holds you down so the rich man can rape you. There's your prosperity, freedom and democracy right there.

Tuesday, December 14, 2010.

What I Have Found

It was somewhere around 2004 that I first ran across David Icke on-line. Someone had posted a video of one of his day-long slide presentations at a theater in England. It was just him up on a stage talking to a full house of people listening intently to his every word.

I started to watch it and was immediately engrossed in what he was saying. He was saying what I was seeing. He was making sense. He was stringing together all of the pieces like beads on a necklace and revealing how they were all connected.

I was so excited. At last, here was somebody talking about the things I was trying so hard to gain insight about. I had done the rounds and never found anything that felt real to me. It was a waste of time going to political web sites, especially the supposedly popular ones. All they did was go around and around and manufacture tangled plates of talk spaghetti. They accomplished nothing. They provided no insights. It was a great big endless taffy pull of "he said—she said" and upholding the same viewpoints and framing of officialdom and big media. It all stayed on the same mainstream acre and never strayed off it. David Icke swerved all the way off it. He was coming at it from a completely different angle.

The first four hours of that video had me riveted. It was straight facts, history, and connecting the dots. I was starving for it. Here was someone who had some answers. I felt so gratified and was not going to budge until I saw the whole thing. At the end of the fourth hour he told the audience it was time for a lunch break and to go eat something and be back for the next part in an hour. I took fifteen minutes and then fired up the next segment. Everything was going great, then all of a sudden he started talking about lizard people. I will never forget how I felt. I was absolutely livid. I jumped to my feet in outrage. It was some kind of sick joke. The guy had made a fool out of me. I was sorry I'd ever had the misfortune to run across this stupid video. I shut it off and walked away.

I went back to sifting through all kinds of things looking for clues, and reading everything I could get my hands on. I had a lot of catching up to do. I was keeping track of what was happening day to day with the absolute intent of knowing who all those people were in congress by name and by face. I was going to watch them and listen to them until I personally knew who they were. At the same time I was going backward in history to understand a great many events I'd heard of but didn't honestly know a thing about. Iran Contra, the Kennedy assassinations, the first Iraq war, Colombian drug lords, senators dying in plane crashes, the Franklin Scandal, the CIA, black ops, false flags, Operation Gladio, Operation Mockingbird, the Cuban Missile Crisis, Kent State, Ruby Ridge, Waco, PanAm/Lockerbie. The list goes on and on. It was pretty damned awful finding out what a bunch of lying, murderous, corrupt men had always been smiling in our faces while doing unspeakable things behind our backs. I was finding out real things, true things that most people didn't know and it was double-damned awful finding out that telling friends about them made me lose all of my friends. They reacted to me as if I had gone over the edge, and they were very impatient with me. They didn't want to hear it. To them, I was sadly misinformed and too dull-witted to know how wrong I was. Or just plain crazy.

It was tough going at the time. The whole country was in the most terrifying pro-Bush fervor. Nobody would dare say anything that sounded like they had a problem with what Bush was doing. The few that did got served up to the likes of O'Reilly who cut them open and tore their still beating hearts out in order to spit on them. Dissent was unpatriotic and any who doubted the 9/11 story or were against the horror and crime of the Iraq war were nothing but scum. It was really vicious. It was the first time in my life I was ever truly afraid. I was afraid of my own government. People who disagreed were in danger, that much was clear. You had to watch what you said and who you said it to, because many people, including long-time friends, were becoming every bit as bad as O'Reilly and every bit as insane.

Combing through leads on the internet and reading from good sources who proved themselves still left a hole where media used to be. I wanted to listen to informed opinion, to hear other perspectives. The media was being torn down. Professional journalists were let go, newspapers bought out, international news offices completely disappeared. There was one perspective on every channel and war was good, the government guys were honest and trustworthy, arresting people for what it said on their tee-shirt was good, and the Patriot Act was patriotic. No photos of flag-covered coffins were ever seen, and we'd for sure find those WMDs eventually. It was an information crisis. There was no information. And the government was allowing media conglomeration like nothing I'd ever dreamed could happen. I found Robert McChesney and watched "Orwell Rolls In His Grave" at YouTube. I saw "The Corporation" and Danny Schecter's "Weapons of Mass Deception" on the spin about the Iraq war.

I read Alex Constantine's investigative article on aspartame and immediately gave up "diet" soft drinks and sugarless gum. Found Betty Martini and Dr. Russell Blaylock and knew I'd never get another annual flu shot. Haven't caught a cold or annual flu bug since. Alex Constantine's piece on the Presidio child care nightmare introduced me to the stomach-turning world of ritual abuse and pedophilia and the usual protection of the wicked by the media and officialdom.

Then I found Jeff Rense. He has covered a heck of a lot of ground and his archives are a great place to get lost in. Jeff Rense gave anybody a chance to have their say, even when they were totally loony. And to his credit, Jeff Rense remains a consummate professional with all of his guests. He is never rude. He never attacks them. He does not go for anyone's throat. He honestly tries to be objective, though sometimes he's not any better at it than the rest of us. That's okay. He's allowed. Jeff Rense's show has drawn back the curtains on a great many things. He deserves credit for his hard work, and I give it to him.

I found Alex Jones and watched his earliest videos. He was definitely onto something. He didn't make anything up. I'd never heard of him before. The first show I listened to was an interview he'd done with a big-time lawyer whose name escapes me; who was coming out with some insider information about official crimes. He seemed to be telling the truth. If what he was saying was true, and it appeared to be true, he was taking quite a risk. I think he's dead now. That happens a lot, I've noticed. I took in Alex Jones' show each morning for several months. This was well before he went pseudo-mainstream, and being so new to this kind of information, I found it hard to blame him when he'd hit the wall. I absolutely give him credit due for shining lights on dark places, but about the time of his first "big" movie it was time to move along. Can I use the word "spazz" without it being a criticism? Because I don't need to criticize the man. It was just time for me to go.

I found Air America and Randy Rhodes and Mike Malloy, but Air America went down the bunny hole. Not much of a loss. I did find Mike Malloy again and hung onto him for dear life for a good while. I feel sincere gratitude for his being such a decent, real man with his values in sound order. He hated war and killing and he talked about Israel and Palestine. He referred to the Bush regime as "the Bush crime family." He was so kind that he took personal emails and answered them too. He even mentioned my very first web site on his show and I got thousands of hits. First class human being Mike Malloy. God love him. And his Kishka Polka too.

I bought Mae Brussel's radio archives and went to sleep at night listening to them. Maria Heller. Greg Szymanski. Black Ops Radio. Radical Radio. Ralph Schoenman. Dave Emory. Red Ice. Guns and Butter. Freedomain Radio. TUC radio with Maria Gillardin (who irritates the crap out of me, because first she tells you what the speaker is going to say, and then he comes on and says it, and then she immediately comes back and tells you what the speaker just said. It doesn't seem to bother anyone else, but it drives me up the wall). Coast to Coast. Jordan Maxwell. Unwelcome Guests. C-SPAN. Indy Media. World Affairs Council. Tons more. I've lost track. I'll bet Google could give me a complete list of everyone I've read and listened to over the last eight years. By now,

Google certainly knows more about me than I do. That's not very helpful to me. More perplexing is wondering how it could be of any use to them, or any of their damned business in the first place.

I found newspapers from all over the world. Canada. Australia. England. Ireland. Russia. Germany. India. China. Jerusalem. Countless web sites. Some did mind-bending, serious research and quietly put it out there to be found. Some were just places to visit, where brilliant people I hadn't found yet were contributors. Some web sites kept their eyes on corporate badness; congressional bribes, er, campaign donations; war crimes; billions blown on corruption, waste and fraud in Iraq; whistleblowers; and the clumsy inbred thuggery of Bush's second stolen presidential election—to name a tiny few. And then there was a literal explosion of political documentaries coming out and a ravenous public hunger for them. My first web site pbsBlog.com was nothing but pages of links to movies about things we'd never see on TV.

All the while the corporate/military/intelligence/congressional complex was relentlessly bunker-busting American freedom and justice. You could not keep up with it. The hostile corporate takeover of America was the real weapon of mass destruction.

Switching through the television channels one day in utter disgust with the dreck and mindlessness of it all, I got all the way up to a little clump of channels in the 9,000 range. I had no idea there was a 9,000 range. These few channels at the end were listed way after the pay movie channels and the pay sports channels and the dozens of radio channels and dozens of foreign language channels in Spanish, Chinese and Hindi. After all that there was a channel for UCTV, and Link TV and Free Speech TV, tucked in-between Mormon TV, Evangelist TV and Catholic TV. Free Speech TV was fundraising. Then Democracy Now came on. I was thrilled.

At the time Democracy Now only had some 130 affiliates picking up the show. It was just Amy Goodman, no Juan. She used to do a War and Peace report, where she actually did reporting on the war. Some of it was really good. She reported on things at the other end of our bombs, and it was eye-opening. I watched it every day. It was quite good for a while, but then it went straight down the tubes.

THE DOT CONNECTOR LIBRARY, BOOK 3

Democracy Now never even mentions the wars anymore. The War and Peace report never mentions war or peace. Fukushima is long forgotten. Nothing of import seems to make it on the air anymore. She won't touch anything of actual relevance with a ten foot pole. And I really don't care if some 93-year-old lady who lived a dream life in some creative career making good money has died. Good. Fuck her. I'm glad she's gone. Make room for somebody else. I don't know her. I don't care. It isn't news. I don't care if that sounds terrible, it's beyond ludicrous. I don't want to hear about orgasms or gay marriage or anything having to do with anyone's bodily fluids. It's not news. I don't care. I couldn't care less about incredibly old people finally giving it up after living totally great lives as writers, dancers or 1940's entertainers, having a ball and wanting for nothing. I don't feel sorry for them. I've never heard of them. It's irrelevant. It's not news. Democracy Now is DOA. They also do totally fake news. They're way gone. What else is new? And just once I wish somebody in the media would give us a Spock frown and say that Mexicans comprising over 50 percent of the US population in less than a decade is somewhat of a shock. It is not automatically wonderful and delightful and happiness in every way. Just once I'd like to see an honest discussion on things like this. I'm not holding my breath. I've moved on.

I also found Patriot radio and hung out there for a while. It didn't take long to realize it was a total crock. It's a game show. If anybody thinks they're going to take America back, they just don't get it. There is no going back. Nothing ever goes back, it moves ahead, for better or for worse. If anyone thinks they can shoot their way out of this, they are very sadly mistaken. Killing your way to happiness is the problem, not a solution. It's a seduction that keeps people distracted or hopped up on Patriot dreams and heart squeezing tales of our saintly founding fathers. It's all a crock. Very effective way to keep people chasing their own tails and missing the whole point, thereby precluding any interference with the game plan.

I don't know how I found Vyzygoth's Grassy Knoll, but it was the first radio broadcast that required me to take notes and do homework. No ads, no incessant breaks for nonstop commercials, just the serious business of getting the picture. His knowledge of history is truly impressive, as is his general knowledge base. He brought in a steady stream of interesting people who were into interesting things and discussed things I was clueless about. Hence the notes and homework. It was great. Just what I needed. He had on guys I'd never heard of, like Alan Watt and Michael Tsarion, and he spoke with victims of organized mind control and horrific ritual abuse. He looked closely at Columbine in an excellent series, and the Port Arthur Massacre too. When Dunblane came up, I already knew the story. The shootings in Norway will without doubt end up on the same shelf. The Informer series on law and the constitution was a kick in the stomach not to be missed. His shows on 9/11 pounded the stuffing out of nonsense and skipped the pointless arguments that amount to nothing. Vyzygoth opened a lot of windows.

Alan Watt is warm and soft-spoken. He is very informative, but in a way that pushes terror and hopelessness. I listened to a lot of his audio before he got on Patriot radio. I don't anymore. I can't take it.

Michael Tsarion is a great speaker, and I've watched most of his videos. He is fearless and walks right over sacred cows without apology. His study of history and his take on things parallels David Icke's story of alien beginnings.

It doesn't phase me at all anymore when David Icke talks about lizard people. I don't have to see anyone morph into a serpent to believe it. It's perfectly clear these people are reptiles. In fact, I see David Icke's story as much the same as what it says in the bible. You say airplane, I say big silver bird. Could we be talking about the same thing? I believe there is an ultimate truth, and I further believe that anyone can find it if they look for it. There are 360 directions to set as starting points. If you and I are both searching for the same thing, and you head to the left and I head to the right, and we spend our lives picking up a trail and becoming one with it ... should we really be surprised to see each other when we find what we've been looking for? Would we need to argue over the reality that your journey and my journey were completely different? Could it matter more how we got here than that we have come to the same place? I would throw my arms around you and be very happy to see you there. We would have much more in common than not.

I have dug into all of these things over the last eight years, always against a backdrop of endless and horrible ongoing war. Now the war is killing ordinary people just like you and me in multiple countries. Average Americans don't know their leaders are seen as barbarians in the eyes of the whole rest of the world. I think they would be truly shocked to realize it. They don't know that American arrogance and disrespect for people in other countries has gone so far for so long that America is now hated. If they were able to see why, they would be heart-sick. They don't know how lied to and manipulated they are, or how cut-off, brainwashed and fearful they've become. They don't see how their leaders are working so hard to provoke world war three and what a bunch of cold blooded bastards they really are. They don't understand that their own elected officials with an entrenched network of insiders set out to break America's back and incite the world into bloody conflagration that will finally be happening here, and not over there. The jobs are gone, the constitution is irrelevant, and the economy is reeling like a drunk about to pass out. None of it by accident; all of it on purpose.

About one year ago, I felt like I had finished a long and complicated crossword puzzle. I put my pencil down. I looked around and saw a lot of other people had finished their crossword puzzles too, some a very long time ago. I could also see that a whole lot of other people were still working on theirs; and a great many others hadn't even gotten started. There was nothing to do but wait for more people to finish. There was nothing left to say. There is no more evidence to drag out and leave in the middle of the road for people to find. All of the individuals and organizations I've mentioned above and many, many more have dug up all the evidence anyone could ever need. The reality of it all is piled up in mountains all around us. Folks trip over the evidence with every step they take. They just can't see it. The moment anyone desires to see it, they will see it. Like the old saying goes, you can lead a horse to water, but you can't make it drink.

So I unplugged from it all and wandered off. I distracted myself. I sat and hurt. I worried. I felt very alone. I stopped paying attention to the violence and filth and lies that never stop pouring into our consciousness. I did not forget about any of those things, I simply stopped carrying them with me. I know they are there. They aren't mine. I don't control them. They are separate from me. They are not a part of me, nor are they joined with me. They are completely foreign to me. If anyone had the power to make it all stop, I am sure they would make it all stop.

I also saw that to directly engage the monster only makes it grow stronger. To engage it is to validate it, to validate it is to give it control over us.

I thought about the future, and I thought about the present. I saw how hard it is for everybody to find a hole in the ice to poke through for air and to discover that there's a whole other world above the ice. I saw how much I've neglected myself and the price I have to pay for that. I asked myself what I was going to do for the rest of my life and realized I had no idea.

It isn't so easy to get angry at people anymore. I know from my own experience how easy it is to get pulled off course. For a while, I was blowing up in a rage over minor things; never at a person, only at inanimate things, and I swore my head off and howled like a dang fool. The angrier I got, the more I raged, and the more I raged, the angrier I got. It was a closed loop of stupidity and pointlessness. There was no satisfaction to be got, only more rage. I would never get to what I needed, which was to not feel angry anymore. I decided to not get angry next time. Instead, I would laugh. Wish I'd thought of that sooner. I can't recommend it enough.

I have gone from thinking that we have so little left to hold on to, to guide us, to help us find a way out of all this to seeing that what we need to hold onto, to guide us, to help us find our way out of all, this is each other. We have all we need. So much struggle and worry and fear, when nobody needs it. Nobody wants it. It is all for nothing. It doesn't have to be this way. We can honestly, truly, just let it go. None of it matters. It isn't real. This is not who we are. I know this in a way that I can't put into words. The static and confusion, the hate and the war, all come from one source: *fear*. Fear isn't there naturally, it is fully and completely imposed on us. It is a prison. The only way out is to love our way out.

I know. What a horribly hokey thing for me to say. The thing is, it is true. All that we know to be good has come out of love. No good ever has or ever will come from any place devoid of love. It is the most natural thing in the world to respect one another and to have empathy for each other. It is normal to love our brother, no matter who he is or where he is from.

God help us if we really feel that love is too hokey for us. If love is too hokey to matter, if love is foolishness, if love is mindless emotionalism, then this party is almost over.

Friday, September 16, 2011.

Beasts Just Wanna Have Fun

Something that is crystal clear to me is that nobody is perfect. All of us are flawed and lost and struggling for the duration of our lives. All of us encounter heartache, pain and disappointment, injustice and misunderstanding, fear and loss and need, and all of us must find a way to cope with these things.

Failure to cope can make things expressly worse, but that often doesn't stop us from failing to cope. Sometimes we decide to not cope out of fear (or stubbornness, or any of your basic seven deadly sins), which invariably causes more of the same trouble, and then we wonder, "Why does this always happen to me?" We end up blaming others for our unaddressed, uncontrolled personal, spiritual and national imperfections.

Genuine coping requires some humility, a recognition that we are not by default always right, nor are our desires and preferences by default the best thing for all involved. When we reject our own need for some humility, we reject our own legitimacy and do real damage to ourselves and others. The problem is that it is often others who suffer for our lack of humility long before we do, if we ever do.

We are all human. None of us are imbued with all-knowing, all-seeing righteousness. None of us are superior to others by sheer virtue of the fact that it is we within our skin. Neither is anyone superior to others because they have a title or wear a uniform or badge. None of these things can magically turn a human being into a superior being. How could they? Good gravy. No external thing can change the basic truth that regardless of how highly we think of ourselves we are still ordinary human beings, imperfect and prone to every human fault and failing that all humans inherently possess. No one is perfect.

There is no such thing as someone who is never wrong. Those who would claim otherwise are full of bull pucky. Yet, there are many who bristle and lash out at any suggestion that they are wrong, that what they are doing is wrong, that what they believe to be factually true or false is not true or false, demonstrably. These are people with false honor. They can seem to be honorable and decent, but they do it selectively, which means that, in fact, they are dishonest and dishonorable. Some tactically use the appearance of decency as a tool to get their way.

From what I've observed throughout my life, a certain grotesque form of self-worship is not uncommon. A whole lot of people obnoxiously and openly express their belief that they are above all others, although when confronted about this, they will usually deny it. They will display self-righteous offense, they will lash out, they will proclaim that their behavior is justified, necessary and right, and that any who disagree are criminals, crazy, evil, or dangerous to society. They are unwavering and insistent that the rules do not apply to them because of their special status among us, whatever that supposed status may be.

Whatever the specifics of their stories, they will never directly answer the question as to how it can be that the rules don't apply to them. This question can never be answered honestly, because there is no justification for the claim or belief that some of us are above the rules that apply to all of us. The bottom line is that society's special people believe that they are entitled to behave in any way they please and may not be held responsible for their actions. They will not hear reason. In fact, they are impervious to reason and cannot be reasoned with, and as I see it, this is the real definition of insanity. This kind of insanity is the very essence of "power."

Power is the ability to do whatever you want regardless of the harm it does to others and to get away with it. I have always thought there was something wrong with people who hunger for power, and it is finally clear to me why. To want this kind of power over others is not sane. It is criminal.

I have little doubt that those who are powerful understand this very well. They recognize the thin line that separates authority from power. There is an important difference between these things. Authority is granted by others, while power is taken against the will of others. If we're talking about freedom, justice, and the legitimate rule of law, then these can only exist in the presence of authority, but they cannot exist under the total control of those in power over everyone's lives.

Authoritarian rule is about having power, and by definition, it is antithetical to freedom. Authoritarian rule despises freedom and demands obeisance, and terrible punishments are wreaked out upon any who have the audacity to hold contradicting opinions from the authoritarians in power.

What we have witnessed of authoritarian abuse of power are things like death squads that torture, rape and murder masses of people, especially poor people and indigenous peoples, because such people are seen as filthy, not human, and useless, and "cleansing" the world of them is necessary in the authoritarian perspective. The authoritarians may also have decided to take the land and natural resources for themselves and don't want to deal fairly with the dirty un-people who live on it, so they simply order them exterminated. Authoritarians construct concentration camps to round up political enemies and other undesirable persons of various cultures, races and religions, because authoritarians fear anyone who thinks differently, does not want to conform, is critical of authoritarian rule, especially if they are influential to any degree or otherwise prefer living in freedom rather than living down on their knees to perpetual fear, brutality and total control over their lives.

These are the things that seriously threaten authoritarian control and vision and are aggressively dealt with in the aim of purification of the people and obtaining everlasting conformity in the kingdom. Authoritarians viscerally hate anything that might undermine their total control over others; and their tendency toward murderous retribution is well documented historically as well as in modern newspapers. This shameless brutality and injustice is the very nature and definition of power, which is why I feel disturbed when I see so many people applauding authoritarian brutality and feeling the vicarious thrill of entitlement and unmitigated bigotry of the powerful to wreak revenge and mass murder on all perceived enemies. Once reached, this state of mind has left reason far behind and is well embedded in the self-licking ice cream cone of insanity. It cannot be reasoned with, and any attempt to do so will likely result in violence against the reasonable.

Few authoritarians are open or honest about their perceived entitlement to have total control over other people's lives. They understand that being blunt about it by simply proclaiming some self-endowed right to control people would be rejected outright by those whom they wish to control, and they would lose their position of power. This presents them a dilemma in that holding power gives them the legal right they need and want to do crime at will and get away with it, but doing crime straight out is not socially acceptable anywhere. So what is an ordinary man in power with raging criminal lusts supposed to do? The answer is as old as it is easy. *He simply lies about it.* The standard authoritarian lie that works every time is telling people that they are under threat from something and that horrible destruction and suffering will assuredly come unless he is allowed to take total control and save them all.

Authoritarian proclamations of entitlement to do whatever they want in order to uphold some supposed higher good, even when what he does is clearly harmful to others, should feel fairly familiar to us today. It is fear mongering. It is insanity. But it works every time.

Authoritarians show a complete and total lack of respect for others, which is also insane. Authoritarians display an abject refusal to put oneself in other people's shoes long enough to understand them, which is inexcusable as well as insane. Technical legalese that exists in support of excusing the inexcusable is completely insane.

When authoritarian rule decimates a nation because it is intrinsically insane, how can we wonder why things are the way they are?

Authoritarians are dangerous, because they refuse to acknowledge the reality that they are imperfect. They believe their station in life erases any imperfections, and so they can never be wrong, no matter how wrong they are. At the risk of repeating myself, this is insanity. It is also insane to believe that you bear no responsibility for the harm you do, when it's clear that no one else could possibly be responsible for your chosen actions. It is complete nonsense. People who are this kind of wrong can't afford to be honest, decent, compassionate or humble. They have no legitimate excuse or reason for doing the things they do. It is all self-serving and rife with depraved indifference to others. It is criminal.

Seeing only one's own self-interests and refusing to consider or respect other people's lives is the very basis of wrongdoing. When people who are not in positions of power lie, cheat, steal or murder, they are prosecuted to the furthest extent of the law. Yet, when those in power commit the same kinds of crimes to a much greater degree, they are lauded and applauded. Instead of their ruthless self-interest being seen as vicious and criminal, it is seen as a sign of strength and single-mindedness.

The problem with single-mindedness, not only in people with power, but in normal day to day relationships, is that when more than one person is involved, more than one mind is involved. Whenever two or more are involved, anyone who becomes so single-minded that they forget or refuse to acknowledge the presence and equal existence of the other minds involved is exhibiting a gross failure of honesty. A total disinterest in understanding all sides in a disagreement can only lead to harm being done. It is unjust, unfair and unreasonable.

Sometimes a failure to empathize is knowing and pernicious, but sometimes it is due to a habit of not trying to see things from the other person's perspective. Often, when the other person's perspective is explained in terms of, "How would you feel if this happened to you?", we can suddenly understand and change our position. It becomes pernicious when we understand and still don't change our position and continue to cause harm anyway. This is standard procedure in taking power over others—you simply ignore their legitimacy and their entire being and do whatever you like.

I have on occasion been taken aback by people I personally know who defaulted into this attitude of self-superiority. They are not only impervious to reason, they reject it with outrage and holier-than-thou displays of temper. They have lashed out with stinging insults and crude remarks with the specific aim of causing hurt feelings and self-doubt, expecting an apology for not seeing them as superior to me and for having my own opinion instead. These are ordinary people who demand subservience to them and an automatic yielding of self to their desire for power over your relationship.

It is shocking and bizarre to go through it, very unpleasant. It cannot end well, it never has. When people become impervious to reason, they are not sane, and you cannot reason with insanity. Other than walking away, I don't know any other way to deal with people like this. Sticking around and trying hard to get them to see reason is pointless. They will not do it. And when they will not do it, you have to walk away.

What possesses some people to automatically expect everyone to see things as they do? The simple reality that more than one mind is involved makes it self-evident that such an expectation is mistaken. Why do some people believe they are so special that no other perspectives are legitimate but their own? What makes them so special? Can they fly? Can they walk through walls? Can they turn invisible? Can they morph into other people or things? Can they turn mice into poodles? Turn lawn clippings into pastry? No. They can't do anything special. They are every bit as human as the rest of us. We are all equal along these lines, none of us have special powers that others don't have. Yet, this simple reality doesn't stop many humans from pretending to be more and better than others; and worse, it doesn't stop many other humans from believing them.

*   *   *

What is a king? What is a queen? A duke, an earl, a prime minister, a president, a pope, a CEO, a general? Are politicians really morally entitled to destroy other people's lives for whatever reasons they claim? Are soldiers really morally entitled to kill strangers because they wear a uniform? Do job titles or sets of clothing make you right when what you're doing is wrong for the whole rest of the world? Are police really imbued with special entitlements to bust down doors without a warrant instead of just knocking, or to shoot unarmed people 71 times in their own home just because they came armed, have special clothes on, and somebody somewhere told them that the very rules they are there to uphold and embody don't apply to them? When you say you're doing something in the name of good, but what you're doing is wrong, does that make it okay? Pardon me, but it does not.

A lot of people want to do wrong things for their own reasons; the definition of wrong being causing harm to others by intent for personal satisfaction. So how can you do harm to others with intent for personal satisfaction and hope to get away with it? There is only one way, and that is to sell yourself and others on the idea that the rules that apply to everyone do not apply to you.

A few common examples:

- You are a special person, called a Queen, because you have a crown and a palace, get paid tons of money, are unaccountable to anyone for your actions or lack thereof, claim inclusion in an elite and special bloodline, and you command a bunch of heavily armed soldiers who will kill anyone who challenges the idea that you're just another lady with nothing special going on.
- You are a special person, called a president, because you live in a famous building, get paid tons of money, are unaccountable to anyone for your actions or lack thereof, and you command a heavily armed military force that will kill anyone who challenges the idea that you're just another man with nothing special about you and that you are indeed fully accountable for all of your crimes.
- You are an important person who is above the rules, because:
  - you have money and power and powerful friends;
  - you are endowed by authority figures with special permission to do things that are wrong and/or you get paid an enormous salary to do them, which somehow makes it right;
  - you wear a badge or are employed by authorities in an enforcement or intelligence position;
  - your work is of utmost importance, according to you, and you're a self-entitled ideologue;
  - it's a national security matter;
  - you're a famous television personality, or a corporate billionaire, or a mega-church TV preacher;

– you have a degree in something and are a lauded, applauded, respected and admired individual in your small circle of experts in their expertise, so if they say you deserve a Nobel prize, even though what you're doing is incomprehensibly destructive, then it must be true.

All of these examples have one thing in common: they all offer and expect unquestioning acceptance of excuses for certain people to do harm to others and get away with it. This is the claim of the special person. The rules do not apply to special people. The rules only apply to everyone else. And you are expected and obligated to be fine with that.

The excuses of powerful people are not part of the normal and usual life experience of the vast majority of people in this country or in the world. In fact, the vast majority of people are told they are powerless and are treated as irrelevant to the interests of those with power. People are trained and convinced to give up their ability to think and act for themselves and to instead allow experts, officials and authorities to do all of their thinking and acting for them, and that they, the weak and powerless, must simply do as they are told or be punished. People are repeatedly told that this is the better way to go and that to not go this way would bring on the end of civilization, raining down anarchy and chaos on us all. Yet, should any thinking person understand what a crock this is and should they stand their ground and refuse to bow down and obey self-important liars claiming impossible authority over the lives of others, they will be harmed by authorities and/or taken away. And most people are just fine with that.

My question of the day is, what is this about? What is this need of some people to portray themselves as more and better than what they are? Why do so many people long for public adulation? What is this extreme passion for idolatry about? And why are so many ordinary people anxious and willing to worship these false gods?

There is no shortage of self-important fakers selling the public all manner of nonsense about their special status in the world. They claim to possess special rights, access, wisdom, information or secrets that nobody else has. They offer to share it only if certain obligations are met.

They offer to sell it. They sell the insane notion that merely on the basis of what somebody has inside their head they are superior or inferior beings, entitled to live and prosper, or entitled to nothing at all. They often will require absolute and total loyalty, obedience, secrecy, and will offer false feelings of superiority and smug insider status. These peddlers of human corruption and weakness are superb salesmen convincing people that obvious lies are truth, when they have nothing special at all going for them. They are nothing and no one special, but people buy it and take it straight to heart.

It boils down to salesmanship, folks, the exact thing that's turned our minds and our country into a corpulent bowl of dumb green violent narcissistic jello. Salesmanship runs the world. Salesmanship convinces people that they want something they don't need or want. Salesmanship appeals to the inner beast, which has no ability to think rationally, it only reacts from the emotional level. Its instinct is to free itself of worry, pain and fear, to avoid discomfort, hunger and need, and to be enveloped in safety, security, affection and plenty. Beasts just wanna have fun.

Like it or not, there it is anyway. What allegedly and supposedly allows us to rise above all of the other beasts on the planet is not free will, it is the possession of a higher, finer aspect of being. One that allows humans the ability to think and reason rather than react, to do math and read, to understand concepts like justice, fairness, truth and lies, and so forth. Where we have gone wrong is in assuming that possessing the ability to use those things is the same as actually using them. It is not the same. It's a bit like that exercise equipment you've got collecting dust in the other room. Just possessing it is not the same as actually putting it to regular use.

By the same token, possessing the capacity for engaging in higher thinking and feeling is not the same as actually engaging in it. Not using these potentials means the inner beast is in charge of our lives and it is not interested in and has no need for higher and finer things like compassion and justice or humility. What does a beast need with any of those things? People who believe in unleashing their inner beast and not forcing it to obey their higher and better will are the self same people who bloviate about survival of the fittest, the law of the jungle, and other such self-excusing hogwash. The unleashed beast has no conscience, and when he kills millions and steals trillions, he calls it success. And we believe him.

A successful beast relies on things other than higher thinking and feeling. If the beast is clever, it can use deception to capture its prey. If the beast is physically small and impotent, it can use poison or deliver a potent sting or bite to take down prey and ward off enemies. If the beast is big and strong, it can use its physical strength to overcome both prey and foe and take whatever it likes whenever it likes from whomsoever it likes. It can kill and not think anything of it.

Interestingly, though, many of the greater beasts of the wild don't use their giant size and strength, cleverness, greater speed or poison to prevail over all others mindlessly and without normal and expectable reasons based on legitimate need. Never do we see a lioness who mindlessly kills deer after deer after deer just to pile them up in a great big pile and gloat over her killing ability. It would make no sense to her. She only kills to eat and she can't eat 200 dead deer before they become putrid, rotting corpses.

Consider also the elephant. A gentle creature that could crush the life out of any human in a second, which instead consents to be used by humans for various human purposes in a mutual agreement. It is only when pushed beyond the limit of patience through humiliating, degrading and unkind treatment that an elephant will finally reach out and squash you like a bug. As the saying goes, even a rattlesnake will give you fair warning before it strikes. It takes a dang good and very understandable reason for a beast to kill a human being. It doesn't necessarily take any good reason at all for humans to kill other humans. Or animals. Apparently, the great beasts of the wild have more going on than we give them credit for. They are not authoritarians. They do not offer excuses for insane behavior. They share the watering hole with all of the other creatures. The only entitlement that spans across all species is the entitlement to take what you need to survive, and that makes perfect sense.

This applies in full to humanity too. The only difference being that humans, being possessed of the ability to use their higher mind, can at minimum show self-restraint and take other people into consideration before acting on their desires. We don't rape whoever we see on the street that is sexually appealing to us. We don't take things from other people or from stores at will. It is this ability to behave in a civilized manner that makes us different from the other animals. But our failure to engage this higher potential undoes civilization and brings on much destruction. When we refuse to control ourselves, let's not pretend we are anything special. We become no different than wild animals.

Our narcissistic human egos want to reject the notion that wild beasts possess any higher qualities. We like to pretend that we are vastly superior to all other sentient beings on the planet. Understand that thinking oneself superior means entitlement to treat those who are inferior to you in any way you like. This is more insanity.

It wasn't that long ago that authoritative official scientific opinion was that animals had no capacity for emotions beyond alligator-brain fear and automatic responses to stimuli. These responses were chalked up to a strange concept they called animal instinct. They even asserted that animals didn't feel pain when you killed them. They weren't even really afraid when you held them down to slaughter them, they were just struggling and crying out mindlessly for no reason; and we believed them.

Scientific authorities were imbued with special powers of understanding beasts that mere ordinary people could never possess, because ordinary people did not have the special official education and training these special authoritative people had. Ordinary people who owned, possessed and worked with animals every day of their lives have long understood that animals have wide-ranging emotions, some quite deep and complex, and that they most assuredly feel pain and suffering. But the scientific authorities ignored the ordinary people's first-hand experience and knowledge and dismissed it as nonsense and drivel and so much pooh-pooh. (So, who are you going to believe? Me or your own lying eyes?)

This pattern of self-excuse for breaking the rules of common decency is rife in authoritarian power culture. Look around and you will see it everywhere. All officialdom is the octopus of power, the arms of power. Officialdom serves and exists to serve power, and I have already established that power is insanity, so officialdom exists to serve insanity.

Go ahead and tell me I'm wrong. You can't. We are drowning in a sea of insanity. Wherever you see injustice and brutality the odds are it is being carried out at the hands of officialdom. This is why cops get away with cold-blooded murder, and soldiers too. Goldman Sachs and Wall Street stealing trillions, getting away with it, destroying the whole western economy, and handing you the bill. Radiation leaks from reactor malfunctions, deadly pills, synthetic food, polluted water and air, destroyed soil, military weapons and equipment that wreak permanent death and destruction all over the world. I'm talking about the clear-cut cases of criminal behavior for which there is no excuse. When the perpetrators are arms of the octopus, they walk free for their crimes. Their crimes will not even be crimes, they will be deemed something else and made okay, even good, fine and noble. A virtual encyclopedia of officialdom's euphemisms exists to support their lies. Everything from "enhanced interrogation" to "collateral damage" and beyond. These euphemisms exist to reframe the horrible into the legitimate and elude prosecution. These are things that no man should ever get away with, and yet they do. Every day.

Official authoritative scientific opinions freed science, industry and the military to treat animals in any way they pleased without pangs of conscience for their cruelty. It has freed science, industry and the military to treat people any way they choose, in the name of whatever phony higher good or self-interest they use as their official excuse for the rules not applying to them. People's homes and land are taken from them, jobs are shipped overseas, the prosperity of the people and hope for the future is decimated and destroyed, thanks to official authoritative expert opinions.

The damage done to health and well-being, to prosperity, to justice, to freedom, to all of us, is carried out by officialdom, not by the ordinary people. When are we going to realize that to blindly trust authority is idiotic? At best.

There is a reason that big industry and science seeks out and aligns itself with power, and it mostly boils down to greed. Breaking the rules of normal human decency to make money is very lucrative and no one is going to be allowed to interrupt a thick and steady profit stream. Today, those who would attempt to shut down cruel factory farms or who agonize over the cruelty lavished onto animals sacrificed to scientific and military pursuits are so threatening to the profit stream that they have been branded terrorists. People who choose to stand in solidarity with poor and politically ravaged people in other countries are also perceived to be and treated as terrorists. That's how greedy and narcissistic humanity can be. But that's only a drop in the bucket, just one example of an ocean of human selfishness and cruelty, all of which has been made holy by the decree of the powerful.

Our American history of owning slaves for personal profit never went away, it has only used time and salesmanship to disguise itself and make itself not only palatable, but pervasive and even highly esteemed. We have all heard that a hard-working person is what defines a person's worth, and we believe it. Don't have a job? Then you are a scum bag and it's all your fault, you're just no good. Good people work so hard that they die at the office. The best workers have no lives outside the workplace, and most people deeply want to be good. They embrace their slavery and see nothing wrong with it. We all want to be good slaves and please our masters. Just try to get out of those ankle chains, friend. You're not going anywhere. Today, there is nowhere to go. There is no underground railroad, the slavers own that too, and it only goes right back to the plantation. Think it through until you see it, it's not hidden. It's all right before our eyes.

*   *   *

The dreadful condition we are in all goes back to authority; who and what the masses of people accept as authority and believe is legitimate authority. There is an unshakable default assumption by many people that all authority is good and that it does what it does for our own good. Because we have this belief, we are not only happy to obey our authority figures, we obey them without question. We believe whatever they tell us. We extend our deep and abiding trust to mere mortals who are every bit as flawed as the rest of us in the unwavering belief that they are never wrong, they never lie, and even when what they're saying and doing stinks and looks fishy and is flat wrong, we tell ourselves that there is a good reason for it, and we keep trusting them anyway. Even in the face of overwhelming evidence to the contrary, of world class wrongdoing, lying, theft, extortion, murder and crime, we still believe they could never do wrong. At least not on purpose.

In America, children never grow up. When they assume adult form, they just become nationalists who transfer their love and undying trust for father over to the state, over to authority figures who do their thinking and deciding and acting for them, and if anyone questions our official authority parents, we get very, very angry. We will kick your ass.

We blindly place our lives in the hands of doctors we don't know from Adam, having no idea if that doctor is capable, was a D student, is a pervert or has a terrible record of causing death and injury instead of helping people get better. To us, every doctor is a pinnacle of perfection, incapable of being a flaming idiot or a crappy doctor, and to question what someone's doctor says only makes you look like a crazy person.

We unquestioningly believe that whatever we see on TV must be true, because they couldn't get away with lying to us. None of us seem to know that it's legal for the news shows we watch to lie as much as they like, no one will stop them and they will never be made to pay a price for it.

Our official state parents are infallible, godlike authorities, and that goes double for the police, triple for the military, and quadruple for experts in medicine, science, business and politics. And if you aren't an officially recognized expert and you know they are wrong and say so, then you are either a lunatic telling lies or a crazy person trying to make trouble. And none of this ever strikes us as slightly bizarre. If the authority figure says it is so, then it's a fact and that's that. If you don't like it, go live in some other country with a dictator and see how you like it. Oh, the irony.

What is authority? What does it mean? Does anyone but us really have authority over our lives? Is authority by definition always right? Is challenging authority wrong? Is it evil? Is it really anarchy? And if it is anarchy, is that a bad thing? I guess it all boils down to who you ask, and I'll throw this in for whatever it's worth, the majority is usually wrong.

Right and wrong are not established by consensus. Right and wrong are indelible truths, in spite of the high volume trumpeting about absolutism and blah blah blah. A tree is a tree is a tree, and right is right, and wrong is wrong, and all of the expert salesmanship in the world can't change that. What salesmanship can change is the way people see things, hence the multibillion-dollar industry called perception management.

Enough! I want to think for myself. I want facts, not opinions, not assertions, not gilded lilies, not TV news mannequins telling me how to feel; just give me the cold, hard, boring facts, and I'll take it from there. I want to hear all sides of a story. I want to listen to first-person accounts, not third, fourth or 55th person retellings of who knows what. I want to hear differing viewpoints and see the outcomes for myself. I want to hear what the accused has to say in his defense and do not find someone guilty who is not allowed to give his side of the story. I do not find someone guilty because authority accuses someone of being guilty. That's just not good enough. Show me the proof, and above all let the accused speak for himself. Give him access to the same media coverage as his accusers so I can hear his side of the story in full.

I don't want to accept anybody else's opinion as my own. I will decide my own opinions and positions and perspectives for myself. I am a work in progress, and if I cannot do those things for myself, then I might as well be dead, for I would not exist in other than physical form. I would not be alive, I would be dead where it matters most, in my mind, heart and soul.

And that is why, folks, I strongly recommend we all consider with true sobriety just who and what authority figures we would lay our lives down for, because the sad reality is that corrupt authority kills people and destroys nations first and foremost. This is not hidden, not today and not throughout history. People often say, follow the money. This is true, but the second part should be, follow the dead bodies, because this will paint the whole picture. This is what reveals false authority.

There are two primary sources of ultimate authority over human lives, and they are the crown and God. It has been so for millennia. The crown is mortal, temporary, weak, imperfect and corruptible. God is immortal, eternal and incorruptible. The crown is by definition imperfect. God is perfect. But the crown conflates itself with God's untouchable perfection and in so doing it makes sheeple out of people and gets brother killing brother in the name of God and country.

This is all driven by expertly delivered salesmanship that preys on emotions, and so it prevails. Emotions become the same as truth when these things have no connection. Emotions are very real, and they are indelible, and once aroused or provoked, they will stand. Emotions cannot be questioned or criticized, because doing so is an unjustifiable attack. Emotions are our most primary property, and we are very possessive of them, and we feel fully entitled to them, because we are entitled to them. What we are not entitled to do is act wrongly because of our emotions; yet, after reaching a point of heightened emotions, we no longer care, and we do terrible things to others, feeling absolutely entitled all the way. The successful conflation of authority with the incomprehensible truth of nature and creation we call God is ludicrous on it's face and a piece of shameless nonsense.

All of the officially sanctioned authority figures we have, meaning sanctioned by the crown, are to be deemed automatically good and right and to be believed and obeyed. The many authority figures in our lives all wear a crown in some form or another; be it a uniform or a badge or a title or a bank account, it is a version of the crown imbued with all the same authority of the crown. The crown excuses the wearer of all liability and responsibility. Wearing the crown makes you automatically right and to be obeyed, and anyone who disagrees is not only wrong, but evil, a scoundrel, a criminal, a thug, an anarchist, a terrorist, someone the media tells the public to fear and hate, and the public fears and hates them on command. The crown is the symbol of being excused from natural reality and getting away with it, and the crown today is donned in many forms. I am not saying that every single person of authority is untrustworthy or bad or wrong; on the contrary, there are some who earn our trust and are accountable for their actions. But the temptation to abuse power is impossible to resist for many mortals, and if the temptation doesn't get you, the peer pressure to conform and threats to ruin your life and career probably will. If that fails, a generous amount of money buys most everyone off. Those last few die-hards, people of virtue, people who stand for natural truth, for the real right and wrong, they are our social lepers whom nobody likes.

The crown is inextricably linked to human sacrifice, and here's why. A whole lot of humans have to die to support the lifestyles and power of the crown and it's octopus, and because the crown is seen as infallibly right and driven by noble motivations and concern for the people, not second to God, but wholly equal to God, then whatever the crown says, wants and does is automatically right. This is how and why human sacrifice carries on without stop and why we are in unending serial wars. This is why we have poverty and injustice and officials and experts who shamelessly and routinely abuse us all.

I will believe that a government is legitimate when there are no more poor people and the prisons are empty. Until then, not so much.

I don't have to tell you how wrong all of this insanity is. I shouldn't have to tell you that false authority is just that, false, and that nobody, none of us, have to live down on our knees before any other mere mortal. If you believe that a mere human being is somehow above you, just watch where their feet are when they walk and you will see that theirs are on the same ground as yours.

I hate special people, I really do, and I am sick of them. I am beyond tired of watching crooks, liars, killers and thieves present their new crowns and don them before us so that they may live their lives above all the rules of God and nature and right and wrong. I've had about all of that I can take.

Never give your trust away for free. Require that it be earned and set your standards high. Your failure to do so will precisely determine the quality of your life and your children's lives, because the ultimate responsibility for your life is in your hands, not in the hands of any authority figure on this Earth. No authority figure, official, doctor, scientist, politician, military officer or institution will ever have to take responsibility for your actions, life, health or well-being. They may claim the force of the law as they tell you what to do, as they demand, command or order you to comply. They may claim the right to prevent you from doing what you need to do to preserve your life and soul. But before you do whatever they tell you, since you will bear the ultimate and full responsibility for your actions, since you alone will have to pay the price if and when things go very wrong, as they often do, you had better make sure it is really something that you truly believe is right. Because the blood stains, regrets and repercussions will forever and only be on your own hands.

Tuesday, April 17, 2012.

Mass Media Illusion

The people I know who are still sound asleep don't see anything going wrong. They are content and distracted, completely disconnected from the world that sustains them. They have no understanding of this. They think their state of disconnection is actually being connected. What are they connected to? The mass media.

Some folks sit in front of a television set for hours every day. They will turn on the TV in the morning and leave it on all day, whether they're watching it or not. The TV is the last thing that gets turned off at night. When they do sit down to watch it, their favorite shows are interrupted every few minutes with groups of advertisements trying to sell products of every conceivable kind.

The ads don't just play once but are shown over and over and over again. The constant interruptions are outrageous and insulting, but they don't mind. They don't feel the insult of it and won't refuse to put up with it. They would never say, "Enough is enough," pull the plug on the TV set and cancel the cable TV account. It would never occur to them to phone the cable company and say they are no longer willing to be abused and exploited by people who want their money and that they're closing their account and won't be back until the commercials are gone. They will probably never just walk away from it all and go do something else instead. No. For the rest of their lives and their children's lives they will sit in front of the TV set for hours each day and night and intake the commercials as if the commercials are a part of the show. As if commercials naturally belong there like unavoidable thorns on a long-stemmed rose. As if commercials are a natural part of television. It's a trade-off they have come to perceive as normal and expected.

Trade-offs in nature are not unusual. Coconuts have impossibly hard shells to break in order to get to the edible white nut inside. Watermelons are unfortunately studded with little black seeds that are not pleasant to bite on. Bees make honey, but they also sting people, and so on. In nature the upsides often come with downsides.

But there is an important difference between coconuts and TV commercials. TV commercials are not a naturally occurring phenomenon. In fact, they are wholly unnatural. There is no human need for them. For the most part people don't like them or want to watch them. After an established fifty-plus-year track record, it is safe to say that TV advertising is pernicious, destructive and hated. Any sane person of sober mind would undoubtedly agree that TV commercials should be abolished.

Television should be for people. It should be about people. It should benefit the public, not the ethically crippled profiteers who feed on our minds, bodies and cash. Television as a technology has the potential to reach, teach and inform. It could also facilitate two-way communication, as opposed to passive one-way output, allowing people at both the local and national levels to actually talk back and to participate and do interesting things, even paradigm-changing things.

For instance, we could use the TV for voting. We could stop voting for personalities that pretend to represent us and instead we could directly vote on the issues that affect our lives ourselves. We could do that and actually have a say in how things are done around here. TV could be a people-empowering technology that makes us stronger, smarter, wiser, more knowledgeable than we have ever thought possible. TV could lift the whole world higher.

But no. Instead, the commercial TV product makes people passive and stupid, disconnected from reality, insecure and covetous. It addicts, disables and disempowers people, turning their brains to mush while making corporations richer through carpet-bombing the human psyche with unmitigated idiocy and scientifically perfected mechanisms to undermine and destroy the capacity of people to think for themselves at all. TV is nothing more than a tool of exploitation of all of our people so that the rich and powerful can get richer and more powerful and maintain an ever-increasing control over all of our lives to an extent that is truly horrifying. It's really quite rude.

When I say things like that to those who are still asleep, they look at me like I'm crazy. They don't deny what I'm saying, they just don't see it as that big a deal. They are sure that they are too smart to be affected by anything on the TV set, programs or otherwise. They feel informed and in control and are not concerned about what I'm saying. By the same token, they don't know anything about the economy or history or what their dearly elected are doing. They often don't even know the name of the vice president or, for that matter, the names of their alleged representatives. They can't name or describe a single piece of legislation that has ever been on the table or was passed into law and don't pay the slightest attention to all things political. They can however tell you all about Bart Simpson, sports, their favorite soft drinks, the Oprah show and their favorite places to shop and go out to eat, what the kids want to buy and have and do, and with rare exception no one in their family ever picks up a book or considers reading or taking a trip to the library. They think I'm funny for even bringing it up.

To them, I am the disconnected one. I am the one who does not see the way and the light. They are plugged into "the happening" as it unfolds each day and is presented to them. They know who's who and what's hot and what's not. They know the latest movie that everyone wants to see and the newest cool cell phone model and all about cell phone plans and costs. They know all of the pop stars and all of the popular songs, the TV shows and TV stars and hottest people and movies out of Hollywood. When they turn on the car radio, they enjoy listening to it, while I can't stand the car radio for two seconds, because it is sheer insanity. Insanity is the norm in this country. Insanity is good. Insanity is fun. Insanity for one and all is the goal and the reason for living. Plug into the insanity and join the insanity collective, and you can be normal too.

Here's the thing. There is no such thing as "the happening." It is all an illusion. It is believed to be real, because it is an ongoing story that people identify with. People live their lives vicariously through identifying with an externally generated stream of illusion. They take their identities, perspectives and values from an externally generated, pervasive, all-encompassing, non-stop, 24 hours a day illusion stream. It feels real to them. It *is* real to them.

Take away the TV set, the movies, the advertising, the pop stars, the radio, shut it all off. Now tell me who you are. Tell me what is real. Tell me what matters now.

A shock of silence happens when the external bombast of the mass media collective is removed from conscious awareness. Attention is abruptly focused within instead of everywhere else except within. In that silence you can hear yourself think. Only in that silence can you hear yourself at all. The question is, can you stand it?

Can you stand hearing your own mind and no other voices? Can you sit in silence and think? Can you bear being all by yourself? Have you ever considered doing something on your own, without anybody else being with you? Does the very idea of being alone frighten you?

If you feel that being disconnected from everything happening out there would be horrible and unbearable and that you'd feel lost and alone and wouldn't know what was going on and wouldn't have the slightest idea what to do with yourself, then I have a question for you. Do you actually exist?

Would there still be a "you" if you were blocked off from all of those external things and other people? Do you exist as a unique individual with your own identity and ideas that come from yourself and are not dependent on what anybody else thinks or says? Who are you? Do you know? Do you know what the meaning of your life is? Do you care about what it means to exist in a world floating in space, or why you are here, or why it matters? Does it even matter to you?

I can't show you proof to support this, but my guess is that most people ask themselves questions about meaning fairly early in life. Around the time we're becoming teenagers we start to wonder about things like why we exist and where we come from and what it all means. This is the time when we stop being Mom and Dad's little acorn, a product of the trees they are, and we start to become a tree of our own.

The first thing a tree has to do is set down roots. Unless and until it can do that it can't do much growing. If the spot it tries to grow its roots into isn't optimal for growth, then it won't become a big strong tree. It might not die, but it will be limited in its growth and will likely come out small and scraggly and unable to produce much, if anything at all.

You are a tree. I am a tree. We are all trees. The difference is that we can decide when and where to grow our roots and, just as important, what we want to use as our life's ground. Whatever we grow out of will be the foundation of everything about us. What we grow into and become is inextricably linked to that foundation. The roots I am speaking of are not physical, they are mental. The roots of our mind will determine who we are.

It's easy to see how plugging into the collective mass media illusion seems like an easy and obvious way out of facing up to and dealing with the questions of identity and meaning churning around in the turmoil of everything else inside us. It's also very difficult to ignore the mass media or avoid it. It's as if there are enormous flat screens floating over our heads at every moment of our lives depicting the ongoing stories, the illusions of the collective. We have no control over what is projected, nor are we a part of its story. We don't personally know any of the familiar people on its screens or anything about them, and yet we feel as if we do know them, and they feel like real and authentic people to us who are somehow a part of our lives. Nothing on the screens are our own story and nothing we see and hear has anything to do with our lives; but there it is anyway, and the people projected there are glamorous and beautiful, wealthy and successful. They are cool, they are right, they are popular, or authoritative, or extreme, or geeks, or they're angry, rebellious, fighting back, lashing out, being stalked by a lunatic with a chain saw, having sex with everybody and anybody; there is always somebody up there to identify with. Whether we know it or not, or like it or not, we will emulate these illusory people. We will dress like they dress and try to look like they look. We will say the things they say and behave as they behave. They are our illusory role models, digital projections who are not even real, but we don't think about that. We just take it in as our reality.

If the collective mass media becomes the soil we put down our roots into, then illusion becomes the foundation that supports our world view. Illusion becomes the source of our personal identity. And illusion becomes what interests us most.

Life is easy to understand, because all questions are already answered, all values are already assigned, and everything is pre-labelled, pre-chewed, pre-discovered and provided. Life becomes effortless. All you have to do is choose. Choose an identity and go buy the accessories that go with it. Life is but a dream.

Nothing in the illusion can answer our questions of meaning, self-worth or true identity. No illusion can supply the real meaning that is the only soil we can grow in. Even our growth is an illusion. Our thoughts and opinions are based on illusions, along with our self-image and ideas about everything in the world.

Our thoughts, feelings and values about these things don't come from our own tree, they come from a tree of illusions, and we are only pretending they belong to us and are us. We will never feel whole or satisfied without answering those questions ourselves. Those questions will be like sneakers in the dryer of our minds, banging around waiting to be pulled out and dealt with. If we ignore them long enough or talk ourselves out of paying attention to them, eventually we won't hear them anymore. If we fear facing those questions, if we avoid them, deny them, or tell ourselves that they are proof that we are not like everybody else and we must hide them or nobody will respect us anymore, then eventually we will learn to successfully block out the noise they make inside our minds.

It is a choice. Listening to our truth within, or choosing the collective mind. We can choose reality and truth and grow ourselves, which is plenty interesting and rewarding. Or we can opt to allow exciting and beautiful illusions to define us. We can let other people form our mind, construct our self-image, think for us, and make us believe that we are no more than what they want us to be. If we allow the illusion stream to define us, then our life is an illusion and we will be entirely unequipped to handle reality when it inevitably rears its terrifying head and vomits into our lap.

Please, if you have kids, pull the damn plug on the TV. Don't let your kids sit in front of the thing morning, noon and night. They still have a slim chance to exist for real, not as an illusion. I don't know what life will be like when nothing is real anymore. The day is coming. In fact, it's pretty much here.

Friday, August 10, 2012.

Politically Correct

Are you, or is anyone you know, *politically correct?* If so, you may want to consider the consequences.

Consequences, you say? What consequences? Well, how about this one. Being politically correct runs the serious risk of you reducing yourself to a junkyard dog for the Thought Police. Are you the property of the Thought Police? Are they your masters? No, you say. I am no one's property but my own. Oh, really? Well, here's a test.

You hear someone saying, "I am against all of this illegal immigration. I absolutely believe, when illegal immigrants are caught, they should be deported back to where they came from." Or, "I can't stand homosexuals. They make me sick. They are all going to go to hell." Upon hearing these things, how do you react? If you are a junkyard dog of the Thought Police, your reaction will be something like this: "Woof! Woof, woof! There is somebody thinking incorrect thoughts! How revolting they are! I despise them! They must be corrected. I will go tell them how despicable they are and let them know they are not okay with me. I am entitled to do this, because my masters told me so."

If you are not a junkyard dog of the Thought Police, your reaction would be more along these lines: "Whether I agree with them or not, everybody is entitled to their own opinion."

Which of these reactions is closest to your own way of thinking? This is no small thing. You may honestly believe that your politically correct opinions are your own, but they may not be. The more adamant you are about your popular politically correct opinion, the more likely it is that your opinion is really not your own. The more intolerant you are of other people's viewpoints and opinions, the more likely it is that you have been brainwashed into holding your politically correct opinion. To put it simply, you have been cultified. You have been Jim-Jones-ed. You are no longer you. You are the property of the Thought Police and will spend years of your life barking at, snarling at, attacking and reporting on anyone you run across who is thinking unauthorized thoughts. Is that really something you set out to be? An intolerant attack dog of the Thought Police?

Do you believe that what other people think needs to be policed? Do you believe that people with viewpoints other than your own are automatically bad? Do differing viewpoints offend you and make you angry? If so, why?

If I like yellow and you like blue, does it take anything away from you? No, it does not. The same is true even if I am a racial separatist. A militia member. A neo-Nazi. A felon. Even if I question the holocaust. Even if I am a Muslim, or an atheist, or a Christian, or a Jew. Even if I'm a liberal or a conservative. The nature of the difference is irrelevant. I can feel 100 percent different about a barrel full of things than you do, and it will not affect you in any way. It does not take anything from you. It does not prevent you from having your own thoughts and feelings and viewpoints. You will retain everything that is rightfully yours. It is not a threat to you in any way when I see things differently than you do.

My thoughts and opinions, viewpoints and beliefs have nothing to do with you. These are a part of my identity and I have every right to them, as much right as you have to yours. My beliefs coexist in this world with your beliefs, there is no problem here. So why then should you feel offended and angry at my rightful opinion? You could only feel offense and anger if you are intolerant of other people's rightful opinions. Your intolerance is a form of aggression against me. You want to use force to try to take away what is rightfully mine. Now, which of us is wrong? Who is harming who?

The simple reality is that everyone has their own thoughts and feelings, and these are not up to anyone else to determine. I feel and think what I feel and think, and so do you. There is nothing wrong with this, it is normal and healthy and necessary. The one thing any of us have to offer is our own unique way of seeing things. It behooves us to listen to each other. If we don't agree, it doesn't mean anything. It is not a reason to become enemies or to fight.

If we try to understand each other's position, we will probably be able to understand why we feel the way we do. Once we understand why certain feelings and beliefs are held, we can see that there are reasons behind them, that it's not just senseless or hateful thinking. It may be misguided or mistaken, but we can understand that if we saw what they saw, we would feel the way they feel. This is not a crime. If we honestly care about justice and peace, then we are obligated to make the effort to understand other people's positions.

Once we understand each other, we can see the bigger picture. We don't have to agree or embrace each other's beliefs. We can retain our individuality totally, but we can at least understand why we feel the way we do. We can see it is not a threat to us. We can simply agree to disagree. We can still be on courteous terms, we could even go out to lunch with each other. This is a good outcome. If we are civilized people, we want a good outcome. We want to be able to get along with everyone we can. All it takes is some tolerance, some respect, and to make the effort to understand why other people see things the way they do. If we do this, the odds of experiencing good outcomes and improved relationships are much improved. We can still respect the person, but disagree with their opinion. We must make room for one another, because the alternative is destruction. Will we kill our way to happiness? It doesn't work that way. It never has and it never will.

If we don't even try to understand someone else, then how can we judge them? If we don't understand why someone else sees things so very differently than we do, then we do not know the whole story. We only know our own side of the story. It is always a terrible mistake to tell ourselves that only our side of the story is the whole story. It is not. As long as there is someone else involved, then they have a side of the story too. To ignore it or dismiss it without listening and apply our judgment to them is evil. That's right. It is sheer evil.

It is evil, because we don't care about knowing the truth. When we don't care about what the truth is, then we are lost in dishonesty. We are dishonest with our own selves. Who can we be without truth? What will we become when we don't care what the whole truth is? Can we become wise and just when we don't care about truth? No. We can only become ignorant and unfair when we care more about protecting our own position than we care about understanding the positions of everyone involved. This is the only way we can get to the whole truth.

But what do we do when somebody is saying something that we strongly disagree with? Until you develop skills like tact and humor, there is only one acceptable way to respond, and that is to shut up. If you are incapable of letting someone have their opinion, then the problem is with you, not with them. They are not doing anything wrong. They are not doing anything *to you.* If, however, you attack them for their thoughts and feelings, then you are definitely out of line. You have no right to batter anyone with your fists or your words. After all, who the hell are you and what makes you better or right or anything else? You have no right to dictate what others must think or feel. You wouldn't appreciate someone doing that to you, would you? Then don't do it to anyone else. If you truly can't tolerate what someone else is saying, then leave. Be polite, but walk away. It's really that simple.

Ostensibly, you hold your strong politically correct opinion, because you want the world to be a better place. But if you truly want the world to be a better place, then you must instinctively know that we can't get there through violence, abuse and anger. We have to learn to accept one another as is and never make the mistake of stepping on people by dictating to them what they must think and feel. They are capable of doing their own thinking and feeling. It is not our place to dictate anything to anyone else. Policing other people's opinions is not our job. Our job is to learn how to handle it. Gracefully. Fairly. Objectively. Respectfully. That is, if that is the kind of world you want to live in. If that is the way you would like to be treated. If it is, then you had better treat others that way, and not just when it's easy, but when it's hard. That's when it matters most. That's how we make real changes in this world, changes for the better. When we are fair with people. When we show respect for people by making human life more important than being right. When we make sure to preserve other people's dignity when interacting with them and don't feel entitled to tear into anyone for what they believe. There is no such right, I don't care what your cause is or how strongly you feel about it.

Understand, this is not about what other people think, this is about *you*. This is about who you are. This is about the kind of person you are. Are you a good and decent person? Then act like one. If you behave like a bully, like a junkyard dog of the Thought Police, then that is what you are. That is not being a good and decent person. That is being oppressive and controlling, judgmental and small-minded. Hello? Think about it.

Letting other people be who they are is the most powerful truth in the world. Let them be who they are. Let each of us decide for ourselves what we think. If we don't do that, if we slam doors in people's faces, if we treat them with disrespect because of their beliefs, we are bringing misery into this world. We are bringing resentment and injustice into the world. We are forcing the creation of separation between equal beings, making some "good" and others "bad." This is wrongful and destructive. It does not make the world better, it makes things harder for everyone. These are the seeds of war. What do you help by planting them? It is so important to show respect to everyone, it is absolutely necessary. That we disagree with them is irrelevant, that is never grounds to treat people with disrespect or cruelty. How could it be? What nonsense. We are not the end all and be all of the world, no one is. We are not special, no one is. We are all equal beings. We all count. Regardless of whether or not we happen to agree or disagree with anyone else, we are still equal beings and we still deserve to be treated with respect.

As long as we can agree to disagree, we can find a way to get along. It is only when somebody somewhere decides they must have their way and refuses to show a basic respect for others that everything comes apart. That is when violence begins. Injustice, cruelty, torture, imprisonment, intolerance, taking sides, name-calling, nasty lies, manipulations—all of the things that tear relationships, friendships and nations apart.

Everyone deserves to be heard. Every side must be given equal time to tell its portion of the story. All sides must be considered before we can draw conclusions about anything. It is far better to assume that everyone is at least partially right than to assume only you are right. When everyone has a valid viewpoint, when everyone is right, we are much more likely to work together to find answers than we are if we refuse to acknowledge that other people actually have reasons for feeling what they do.

Political correctness is a lie. It is exactly the opposite of what it pretends to be. Political correctness is a method of controlling the minds of others. It is oppressive and deceptive. It turns people into monsters. It broadcasts orders to attack others, to behave with incredible selfishness and intolerance, it makes people feel entitled to behave rudely. What is "correct," anyway? Correct is different depending on the people looking at the equation. To be so arrogant as to presume that you are automatically correct and no one else can be correct is dishonest at best and fascistic at its core. If you believe in freedom, then being politically correct is a total contradiction. It can only be one or the other. Either you believe in freedom or you believe that people must be controlled by force. Which is it?

If what someone else is saying makes you want to get in their face or hurl labels at them like "racist" or "denier," then you must stop yourself and ask yourself one question, "What's it to me what somebody else thinks?" Is it your problem what they think? No. Is it within your control to make them think otherwise? No. Is it your right to dictate to them what they should believe? No. Are you responsible for what anyone else thinks? No. Then why are you carrying their luggage? Let them carry their own luggage while you relax. It's not yours to worry about.

You must accept that you have no power to change anyone but yourself. You cannot make people see things differently, at least not by attacking or disrespecting them. They will definitely not consider your perspective if you show no respect for theirs. You get back what you put out, and if you put out a brick in the face, don't expect hugs in return.

It is also worth questioning why you feel the need to be so controlling of others. If you're losing friends over disagreements in matters of opinion, maybe you need to look at you for a change. Maybe you need to mind your own business instead of somebody else's business for a change. Why do you expect anyone to embrace your position in lieu of their own when all you do is come at them with insults and disrespect? You are only throwing gasoline on the fire when you do that, and yet you expect them to forfeit their honest beliefs and step over to your way of thinking? Is that silly or what?

No matter who anyone is or what they think, treat them with the same respect you want to be treated with. It is never about them, it is always about you. Your behavior is all you have control over, are you doing your best? Really? Is showing off your intolerance for others something to take pride in? Or is understanding that everyone has equal rights to their beliefs something to take pride in? I'd say it's the latter.

Anyone can be intolerant in the name of some greater good. Just like the Spanish Inquisition. Be careful who your masters are. If you don't, you will soon find yourself steeped in hate and self-righteousness even as you claim to be against them.

Bottom line: don't ever let anyone else tell you what to think. Think for yourself. And when you get to the point that you can defend someone else's right to their opinion, even though you disagree with what they're saying, then you'll have done more to do good in this world than you'll ever know.

Thursday, August 9, 2012.

Broken Angel

It was perfect weather for a parade, and on a warm and sunny Saturday afternoon, Main Street was packed with people. The sidewalks on each side of the roped-off street were still crowded, even though the main parade had just ended. The people were now waiting to see a man.

The man was a famous celebrity, not an actor or a singer, but a businessman. A very wealthy businessman who didn't actually earn his wealth, he stole it, as is the tradition. Reputed to be heartless in business dealings, he was personally responsible for thousands of people losing their jobs and homes, at a time when jobs are no longer being replaced with new ones. He ransacked pension funds, spending the money on slickly contrived illegal investment schemes that brought back a thousand times his investment, and laundered it to offshore banks. He then filed bankruptcy, and thousands lost their entire life savings. He was quite proud of himself.

He gave no thought to destroying lives or families, to the suicides of overwrought hopeless people, to mortgages foreclosing by the tens of thousands, or any of the pain he caused.

This man was unconcerned with any effects his business dealings had on people, he cared only about his profits and success. One of the chief architects and key players in the devastating ricochet of mergers and buyouts of the 80s, he continued to increase his wealth with the advent of outsourcing. Downsizing, streamlining, anywhere there's a corporate buzzword, he'll be there.

He's been in too many investment scandals and frauds to count and has gotten away with all but one of them. There was a token indictment, a trial to appease the outraged masses, and a guilty verdict ordering him to pay $250,000 and spend 15 years behind bars. He did six months in a country club penitentiary where he had every amenity including an office to enable him to continue his wheeling and dealing behind bars. It was hardly a punishment. And while $250,000 sounds like a lot of money, to him it was nothing. He got to keep the rest of the 26 million he'd gained committing the crime.

Through years of privileged access to money and the corporate aristocracy he'd accumulated a personal fortune of nearly ten billion dollars. He has never known a day of his life that was not extremely comfortable. He grew up in great wealth. He is well familiar with its comforts and denizens, he knows the ropes and the connections. This is his norm, and he could never tolerate anything less than the absolute best of everything.

Newspapers lauded his capitalist skills, doting on his contributions to the economy, which he so busily and efficiently pillaged. He's a familiar face on the largest corporate news shows, mainstream financial talk shows, and even public television. He's a darling of both the establishment and the government who never miss an opportunity to grovel and adore him, as though he were a hero. He is also known to have connections with organized crime.

This man has never done a single thing for the people of this country; in fact, he is arrogant and open when expressing his depraved indifference to those he deems beneath him. He feels no inclination whatsoever to "give back to society." He couldn't care less about society. In fact, he believes society owes him everything and that it is his right to pillage and destroy whoever cannot defend themselves against him. But he does enjoy the groveling and attention of lesser beings, and that's why he came.

In spite of his well-known destruction of the working class, his felony records and cut-throat capitalism, crowds gather to see him wherever he goes. He charges exorbitant fees to be a guest speaker, and he stays quite busy doing it. Afterwards people always cue up to excitedly shake his hand and ask for his autograph, grinning at him as if he were a hero.

He is one of the top 100 people directly responsible for the total devastation of this country, but the people worship him. They want to see the rich man, the wealthy man who lies, cheats, defrauds, and has stolen his way to over 800 million dollars of personal wealth.

His chauffeur-driven black limousine is only minutes away from arriving on Main Street. At this time, the waiting crowd is subdued, yet attentive. Many are hoping to be the first to glimpse his limousine when it turns onto the street. Eyes and heads occasionally glance to one end of the street, and then the other, then return to their conversations.

It is 3:59 PM as a pleasant, barely noticeable breeze gently brushes over the crowd, then dissipates. It is just at this moment that another man is beginning to round the south corner of this street. In a matter of seconds he will stumble on to the street and stop at dead center where he will be seen by everyone. This man has no idea where he is, nor is he even aware that there is a parade. He is in far too much agony to notice. He needs help.

He had been mercilessly beaten during a night in jail, not for committing any crime, but just for being in the wrong place at the wrong time. The police had arrived and arrested him without asking questions, and because he is homeless, dirty and hungry, they treated him with utter contempt, berating him and trying to beat a confession out of him with various forms of cruelty and torture, some of it painful beyond description. This had gone on for hours. He'd been deprived of clean water and food, and even the use of a toilet. Now he was swollen and bruised and in obvious pain.

Less than five minutes before, he'd been released from the jail, unceremoniously booted out onto the street once they'd decided he had not committed the crime, without so much as an apology. He was not offered any assistance by the police. They disdained him and didn't hide that fact. Bruised and betrayed, starving and violated, he had slowly walked a block from the police station. He was exhausted and in too much pain to go much further. He needed to find a safe place to lie down and sleep, but he was very hungry. He desperately wanted to be in a safe place, to clean up, tend to his wounds and sit down to a decent meal.

Standing in an alley way, in the giant cold shadow of a great gray building, he studied his surroundings. He needed to make sure no one was looking. Then, bending down he removed one of his battered shoes. Carefully he felt inside it for a loose flap of fabric near the heel, then opened it and gently pulled out a single tightly folded fifty dollar bill. It was all he had in the world. It was given to him by a kind passerby a month ago, an act so charitable and generous that he couldn't bear to spend it. He thought it could be his lucky charm, a sign that things would soon change for the better. He'd decided to keep it hidden away and promised himself he would not use it unless he was in truly dire straights. This qualified.

His hands shook from hunger as he wrestled the bill from the shredded shoe lining. He was so glad that it was still there that he felt like crying. He resisted the urge to break down, it wouldn't be seemly for a veteran; because in spite of society's disrespectful treatment of this war vet, he still had his self-respect. He did not judge himself by his clothing as they did, and he would not allow his pain and inability to understand his fellow man's attitude toward him keep him from retaining his dignity. Such as it was.

He now replaced the shoe onto his bare foot with one hand, and holding the fifty dollar bill in the other, he glanced down the street looking for someplace to buy food. He could get a cheap hotel room, just for one night, to give himself a soft place to lay down and a single night to begin to heal his battered body. He could actually get some rest if he didn't have to stay awake all night to protect himself. He'd be out of danger in a small room with a locked door and a sturdy brace.

It sounded very good to him, so he headed for just such a place. Hotel Fancy was dirty and run down and rented by the hour, day or week. It was host to prostitutes and johns, drug addicts and suicides. It was a likely place for the homeless to go whenever they managed to beg enough money to buy a room for a day or two and get a rare, coveted hot bath. With real soap and everything.

His footsteps were slow and shuffling, every move he made hurt. But as he walked, he imagined hand-washing his clothing in the hotel sink, then being able to have clean clothes again, to wear the next day. Things were looking up, he told himself. After a hot bath, his hair would be clean and he wouldn't smell so bad, and that would make it easier to go into a store or restaurant to find some food. He wouldn't get run out so fast. He might actually get something decent to eat.

Lost in thoughts of a real hot meal, he didn't even see who stabbed him. His eyes were fixed in horror on his fifty dollar bill as it was grabbed roughly from his weakened grasp. It slipped through his fragile fingers as the knife blade retracted from his left lung and back out of his body. Sadness and anger burst forth in a single soundless cry, "No!..."

The feeling of sadness and disappointment literally overwhelmed him as the pain of the knife wound hit, changing his hopeful expression into an open-mouthed grimace of desperation and agony. It was almost too much for him to bear. Now he was having serious trouble breathing.

His military training told him he had to get help, or he would die, but he was out of the sight of passersby. He did not want to die. More than anything he wanted the chance to keep on living and regain his pride, to be welcomed back by the family that discarded him after the war, to prove his worth and be loved, to have a normal life again. It was what he wanted more than anything else in the world. If he couldn't make himself seen, he would die where he lay.

With all of his strength he struggled to his knees, and then to his feet, leaning on his outstretched arm, his shaking hand flat against the building. Then, turning, he grimaced with pain, and saw he was only a few feet from the corner, the corner of Main Street. Someone would surely see him from there.

He went for it. The blood loss made his already weakened condition all the more fragile, and his head spun as he staggered for the brightly lit patch of sidewalk ahead. He had to make it. He just had to.

On Main Street, the crowd was beginning to grow restless. A chorus of chattering voices echoed between store fronts as the sunlight began to dim. The clock on the bank tower chimed the hour, it was 4 PM, precisely. It was at this exact moment that he stumbled around the corner and out into the middle of the street. A street lined with expectant parade goers, people who were waiting to meet one of the richest men in the world.

All eyes turned to him immediately. The hum of voices was punctuated by whispers and gasps and a few pointing gestures. He felt himself losing consciousness, and as he fell to his knees, he looked out at the faces, which were no more than a blur, and he whispered, "Help me... Please..." He fell face forward onto the dark pavement, then lost consciousness. He was so afraid he was going to die.

It was now that the crowd could finally see his blood-soaked back. But no one in the crowd made a move to help. They were too appalled, too concerned that their involvement would prove to be an inconvenience, and he was too disgusting.

His face had barely hit the pavement, when at the other end of the street the very wealthy man came round the corner in his chauffeur-driven open-top limousine. It gleamed in the dappled sunlight. His gorgeous-tailored Italian suit was made of a soft, silky deep blue material that shimmered each time he moved. His perfectly shaped padded shoulders and the perfect all-over fit of this expensive handmade garb made a stunning and strong first impression. The blue of his eyes matched the blue of his tie, which had tiny golden stars woven throughout in a sprinkle pattern, and they were made of 24 karat gold.

His gold watch glittered out from under his shirt sleeve as he raised his right arm to greet the crowd while flashing a perfect white smile, which was just as fake as his thick brown colored hair. The limo slowed to a full stop, and he stood and raised his other arm in the air making a "V" shape. V for victory, the name of his latest book. He looked fabulous, quite impressive, and very wealthy.

The marching band began to play, and he just stood there like that, smiling, receiving hand-thrown hailstorms of colorful confetti from the crowd. The people on both sides of the street went wild, cheering and applauding him. Many began to rush toward his car, surrounding it and calling out his name. There was much excitement and fuss as the music blared, and it beat out the perfect rhythm to match the crowd's exuberance. The once calm street had now become a celebratory circus of idol worship.

A pretty young woman leaned into the car to hand the rich man a pen, then excitedly asked him to sign her copy of his book. As the man complied with exaggerated gestures, much to her giggling delight, at the other end of the street, the cold, hungry, beaten and stabbed veteran died in the street, alone.

Monday, January 14, 2008.

The Answers

Everywhere that I have ever been in America, there is a sincere belief in the notion that The Answers are out there. Answers to all of life's questions. Not just any old answers. The answers I'm talking about are The Answers, the only real, legitimate, for sure, the buck stops here, no matter who asks the question, this is the answer. Answers. *The* Answers.

There can only be one "The" Answer for every question, and that is the one everyone wants. Because once you get The Answers, you have it made. You're good to go. You can't be wrong about anything. Life is a piece of cake, everything works, you glow in the dark, and everything you do is right, forever more, yahoo.

Unfortunately, we're born without The Answers, and we soon realize we'll never get The Answers unless we go out looking for them. And they are always "out there" somewhere, never right under our own noses or anywhere else we can find them easily, or come up with them ourselves. That is especially frowned upon. (And there in lies *The* Problem, IMHO.)

Even though they're in widespread demand, The Answers are tricky to come by. They're mysterious, ethereal things, lurking secretively in faraway places. Many have searched far and wide, and many believed they found the darn things, and they told everyone else all about it out of the kindness of their hearts.

Yet, for all the millennia that humans have been searching for The Answers, no one as yet has passed Go, collected $200 and become the undisputed winner of the title, "The one who finally found The Answers." Hasn't happened yet. So, even though there are many who claim to have The Answers, the search is still officially on. The *real*, absolute, hands down, genuine "The" Answers are still out there somewhere, ostensibly, waiting to be found once and for all.

The Historical Search for The Answers

Every culture throughout known time has recorded their own stories about people who have gone in search of The Answers. The people in the stories have given their entire lives over to their journeys, traveling to all of the far-flung places of the Earth. They explored all four corners, crossed every ocean, slogged across every desert, sat in every cave, have conversed with every kind of talking animal, had amazing encounters with countless half-human/half-something-else creatures, met bizarre physical and nonphysical beings or forces, some with amazing powers, some with none, and it all became a part of the stories describing those journeys for The Answers. Whether memorized or written, the stories have been passed down for generations as a gift for future seekers of The Answers so that they will be informed that somebody who went before them already found all The Answers and they must not bother going themselves. Apparently, it is considered very disrespectful to start fresh and explore the world and life for yourself and find out what you can find out on your own. In the olden days that was cool, but not so today. It is very uncool today.

History's real or mythological seekers of The Answers have been painted in the most glorious terms. Never were there more pure-minded, noble-hearted, upright or brave people—always men—who walked the face of the Earth. Reading their stories, you are sure you could never hold a candle to them. They were so honorable and dedicated that they deserved to find The Answers. It often got very tough for them, but they never gave up, no matter what; nothing could detour them from their goal. They endured the worst kinds of hardships and deprivations. Nearly killed a dozen times or killed in the end, they were driven by the all-consuming need to know the truth. According to the stories, they usually found The Answers, and from their discoveries all manner of great and small Answer Franchises have come into being.

The Modern Search for The Answers

Answer Franchises have sprung up all over the world, and they are wildly popular, because they have The Answers, that's a widely accepted fact. Religious, political, medical, educational, scientific, fashion, hipness, ecological, musical, pop culture, entertainment, sports, you name it—they're all there, ready and waiting to give you The Answers to all of your questions. We find Answer Franchises to be incredibly helpful, because we can't all go off trekking to the lost jungles of Borneo, where The Answers would most likely be, or they'd be buried somewhere under 14 miles of petrified Swiss cheese under some obscure European meadow, or painted on a cave wall, or hidden in a long-lost pyramid, or etched on a clay tablet, or sewn into the label of your underwear—who knows, the point is they are darned hard to find, and the bottom line is, people have to have them. Answer Franchises meet the needs of a much rushed, overworked, somewhat dippy public who has come to rely on them almost entirely to make all of the most important decisions of their lives. And most of the unimportant ones too.

Now, some people don't care so much what The Answers are, they're fine with whatever everybody else is believing. The important thing for them is just to be recognized as a member of an established group, which is generally accepted to be in the category of those who claim to have The Answers. Other people need more of a hands on, interactive exploration of the Answer Franchises available to them. They must go to every Answer Franchise they can find, wanting to test-drive them all before deciding which Answers they like best. It's a lot like going to Benihana, except it's not necessarily Japanese, and you're not going out for dinner, but everything else is pretty much the same. Let me explain.

Attaining Enlightenment

You go in and take a seat around a big table, which has a special reserved area at one end just for the franchise operator, then everyone sits around waiting while looking at the pretty lamps and commenting on the decor and the atmosphere and how crowded it is or isn't, and sometimes visitors share tales of previous trips to the franchise or relay stories they've heard from others. Some are old hardcore members, who are generally stand offish, others are nervous newbies anxious to try it, others are stubbornly dubious that there will be any real answers here, and so on.

Everyone is waiting for the franchise operator to come out, because that's where The Answers are. They're not in the Answer Franchise building, you can sit there for three weeks and not get any answers, it's only the franchise owner who has The Answers, and if you want them, you gotta get them from him. So it's always a big deal when he comes out, everybody claps, or they stand up, or they sit cross-legged, or they fill out a questionnaire, or they play Hail to the Chief, or they take a seat in the waiting room, or they sit in front of a moving picture and sound box; it's a little different at every franchise. The bottom line is, the people are ready and facing front, waiting to hear The Answers.

The chef finally appears, wearing the garb of the franchise, always very nice stuff, not the usual street attire in many cases, and takes his place at the reserved, off-limits to others, special end of the table, and then, with well-practiced moves, he proceeds to dazzle the onlookers with his many brilliant skills, which proves that he has The Answers. He often tosses a whole fish into the air, and by the time it comes back down, he's managed to julienne it six ways from sundown and get the skin off too, then he effortlessly fans the pieces out like a deck of cards; perfection.

Now that everyone is duly impressed, he asks everyone which answers they seek and then he proceeds to prepare their answer plate, giving them samples of strange and unusual things, which he presents as The Answers. It's a splendid show filled with much mystery and surprise. Often there are tears and weeping, sometimes there is laughter, even applause, but no matter what, all eyes stay on the franchise owner and his very splendid show. After every plate is filled with an impressive arrangement of answers, the people take them in, sometimes with discussion, more often privately, some with thinly-veiled revulsion, others with gratitude, and when everyone has had their fill, they pay the bill and go on home.

If you decide to become a member of that or any other franchise, then you simply need to show up there to get all of your needed Answers, and voilà, you'll be treated to a show, get answers to questions whether you asked them or not, pay the bill and go on back home. You're in the know now, by golly. This is how it's done and how it's been done for a bajillion years. Everyone gets a membership with an Answer Franchise, then they become instantly Enlightened for the whole rest of their lives.

Availability and Self-Teaching

As to choosing the Answer Franchise best for you, sometimes there's not much choice in the matter. There may be only one major brand for a whole vast region, so most everyone is a member of the same Answer Franchise. The individual franchise outlets can be quite different, but they will still serve up the same menu items with some minor variations, and this is considered acceptable. It's only when the variances become a little too different that real problems can occur that can split entire nations, and even families, right down the bloody middle.

Often there's a handbook given out to everyone who joins an Answer Franchise, in case you can't wait to get all of The Answers. You can technically get all of The Answers from the handbooks, but it's not really recommended, because you have to be a franchise owner to get it right, you see. It's easy to misinterpret the handbooks and go off making a fool of yourself, because you don't understand the special ins and outs of Answer recognition and interpretation. It is strongly encouraged to depend on the franchise owner to do all interpretation for you, self-teaching is too error prone. However, some Answer Franchises welcome group participation, though most often they strictly forbid it. In any case, it's quite normal for the members to not even bother reading the handbooks, even though they own one, because they'd rather get it straight from the horse's mouth. It really feels like *The* Answer when you hear it spoken in real time, directly to you.

Doubt

There is one noteworthy drawback to Answer Franchises, however, and it bears mentioning. No one is ever allowed to question The Answers they are given, no matter how ineffective, unhelpful, unjust, illogical, unproven, unsubstantiated, downright hurtful or obviously wrong they are. Doubt is forbidden at all Answer Franchises, it can get you in a lot of hot water too, depending on the Franchise.

There is a direct relationship between how high and mighty any given Franchise is and its untouchability. A general rule of thumb is that the more wealthy the franchise is, the more powerful it is. The lesser ones can't do much to hurt you if you go around saying things like, "These people are phonies and liars who should be in prison." The larger ones, however, who are the ones most likely to be phonies and liars who should be in prison, can and will come get your ass if you get a little too loud or if too many people start paying attention to your messages of doubt. Doubt of any kind directed at a Major Franchise owner or member will often result in a cold shoulder effect that will dismiss you, discredit you, and eject you from further participation with that franchise.

Conversely, you could be legally forced to comply with a franchise you wholly reject, which is very scary, to say the least. Answer Franchises are serious business. Just because they'll let anybody in doesn't mean they're flexible about anything. They aren't. If you express doubt, you'll be treated to the same contempt given to any non-Franchise member, which is always entirely unpleasant and can even be deadly.

Probably 75 percent of the people in any given country will tell you they are subscribers to, or members of, one or more of the most popular Answer Franchises in the region, but there always remains the pesky remnant, the other 20 percent or so who blow off the Answer Franchises as being silly and made up. Such persons often cause serious upset by saying things like, "Your answers are wrong," or "There is no proof that your answers are The Answers," or "There is no such thing as The Answers," or "I like to come up with my own answers, thank you very much." When they say things like these, they are never embraced. On the contrary, they get lots of hissing and foul language and are often accused of being child molesters or otherwise dangerous, unsavory and untrustworthy, without any evidence to support such horrible accusations ever being provided.

When an individual lacks membership in the most wildly popular

Answer Franchises, it is apparently incredibly threatening to franchise owners and members alike who have been known throughout history to the present day to become downright violent with anyone who shows disinterest, disrespect, or who expresses doubt about their personal franchises having The Answers.

People invest a great deal of their identity in their belief that they possess The Answers through their chosen Answer Franchises, and someone coming along and saying, "My answers are correct and yours are imaginary," or "Your answers are not The Answers," is almost the same as saying, "You are too stupid to live," or "You are naive and would believe anything you were told by an authority figure," either of which, were they true, would be deeply disconcerting.

The major Answer Franchises offer a good deal of protection to their members in the face of any doubters coming around. There is might in numbers, and this is no exception. Franchise members can be counted on to come together in solidarity to protect their claim that The Answers they get from their franchise are The Answers for sure. It doesn't matter at all if they're wrong or right, that's all irrelevant. No proof is offered to disarm the doubter. It's much simpler than that. The most dependably common response to doubters and miscellaneous disrespecters is to attack and destroy anyone who says such things. The Gang Attack and Destroy Method eliminates any possibility that the doubters are right. Well, it doesn't do that really, but it does shut them up so everyone can get back to their Answer Franchise and feel comfy and secure in the belief that they have The Answers.

It's that insecurity, that terrifying idea that The Answers are out there somewhere and we don't have them that makes people so unbearably uncomfortable. Insecurity is so horrible that anything that must be done to avoid it is by necessity all right. Even if it means the organized mass serial killing of perfect strangers in faraway places, it is acceptable; it becomes a matter of honor, because it defends our version of The Answers. It guarantees our continued sense of security, which does not apparently come along with having The Answers. Instead, it comes along with clubbing other people to death who have different Answers than our own. In all Answer Franchises, "they" are always wrong, which makes it okay to kill them; in fact, we're doing them and us both a big favor. Their wrongness is polluting our rightness, and that's just rude. Who needs it? The end justifies our need to not feel insecure about The Answers we happen to have.

For many, there is nothing worse than not having The Answers. Existing in real time like everybody else and being on your own journey is too terrifying a thought. Having The Answers feels like someone's got your back, you won't be as hurt when you fall, and random bad things won't happen to you unless there's a good reason, and if they do, they won't be as bad as they would be without you having The Answers.

Having The Answers means you are doing things right, which makes you feel legitimate every day, no matter how much of an ass or a jerk you may actually be. It also guarantees your acceptance into the very best neighborhoods in the afterlife, which are reserved only for those who are right here on Earth. When you are so right in life, then when you die, that rightness is your automatic backstage pass to the best that death has to offer. That's all nonsense, of course, but this nonsense is so strongly desired that standing between it and someone who needs it will get you mown down without hesitation.

Acting like you have all The Answers is also perceived by many to be a status symbol that elevates someone to "better than you are" status. Many people otherwise lacking genuine self-worth or any meaningful purpose in life will glom onto this aspect of being seen to have The Answers very quickly, and they never let go. Many go on to become Answer Franchise Owners and Operators themselves, and because doubting The Answers is strictly forbidden, there is literally no chance at all that they will ever be discovered to be every bit as devoid of The Answers as everyone else. It's the perfect gig for those who don't mind being revolting inside.

So realize, this is no small thing. It's a real biggie. It's such a biggie in fact that it has become the template by which we get all of our answers today. It's a well-established system, it's familiar and comfortable, and it completely eliminates the need to get up off your ass and get your own answers for yourself. Plus, it eliminates any nagging feeling that The Answers you are given should probably be verified. It eliminates the need for your answers to actually be correct, which removes decades of loathsome self-exploration and questioning to achieve balance, maturity, and a philosophy of life based on reality, and a value system that is genuine. That's just too much work, and face it, why engage your own brain, soul, spirit, creativity and life energy just to get The Answers, when they're already in a local Answer Franchise right down the street from you, ready and waiting in convenient, easy to receive standardized formats? The work's already been done for you! And there are bona fide Answer Franchise Owners and Operators all over the place these days. Why wouldn't you take advantage of it? Everyone else does.

Medical Answer Franchises all have certified Answer Franchise Owners and Operators, licensed by the state, so wow, obviously they can't be wrong about anything. How crazy to look into your own health yourself or be responsible for your own education, or political beliefs, or determine your own opinions or actions about anything, when certified, bona fide Answer Franchises are everywhere you go.

It leaves you free to use all that creative energy and critical thinking ability for really important things, like filling out tax forms, or working for someone else who will get rich off your labor while you don't, or choosing a movie, or memorizing all the titles for every season of *Star Trek,* or finding shoes to match your purse, or figuring out how to cheat on your wife without her catching on or the other broad finding out you're married.

Those are the kinds of things we need to use our time and energy for. After all, what's more important than our immediate carnal and empty ego gratification?

We need to look right, and there are Answer Franchises to tell us how to do that. We need to have certain haircuts and shoes and jobs and go to certain schools and engage in certain leisure activities, and again, the Answer Franchises are there for every little thing in life, so you never have to figure anything out for yourself. It's just a matter of what appeals to you most. It simply can't get any easier or be more efficient or more guaranteed to ensure your security.

You can always be right, even when you're wrong, have all The Answers, and come off as slick as a rainy road just by utilizing all the best

Answer Franchises, local and global, because the whole world is now yours to access in this modern age. Could it get any better than this?

The only question I have is this. If someone feels too inadequate to the task of finding The Answers by themselves, if they feel more secure accepting as true the prefab pay as you go Answer Pack of someone else—then how can they be sure they're qualified to decide who has The Answers or that The Answers they're being given are in fact The Answers?

I guess it should be self-evident that being right isn't all that important to Franchise members. Being really really right simply boils down to majority opinion, consensus reality. And when the Franchise owners and operators join hands and proclaim each other fabulous and credible, that appears to be the hot ticket to *The* Truth.

Somehow, if it turns out that in the end they were wrong or they were liars, we'll still all be off the hook, because we weren't responsible for what they told us. How could we help it if they lied and people died? That's not our fault, we were only following orders. They were experts, they were overwhelmingly accepted by almost everyone, they were highly acclaimed in their fields, they had the most famous faces in Hollywood, they looked like they knew what they were talking about, they wore white coats and had stethoscopes, they had grand titles and status, they were on the biggest cable news channels, they were seen on television all the time, they were rich and making huge salaries, they went to the most prestigious universities, they were democrats, they were republicans, they were the president and the vice president—who would have ever expected people like that to lie?

Oh, come now. Who could have ever expected people like that to do anything *but* lie? When it's *that* easy to take over the minds of millions, you almost can't blame them for trying. When it's also so very lucrative, in the end it would be downright irresistible for them.

The whole world subserviently obeys the Grand Franchise Owners who are able to create a planet made to order in their own image without any fear of ever being made to account for what they say or do. Herein lies the oldest most guaranteed recipe for corruption. It's flat unavoidable.

The blame for our own ignorance lies in our own hands. Where else could it belong? Who is responsible for our lives? We are. Directly, ultimately, inescapably. That's not what they're saying in the Answer Franchises. It's one of The Answers people need most, but will never find out there.

Monday, January 14, 2008.

The Law

We Americans are obsessed with rule-following and the law to the point of ignorance. We think of rules and laws as something from on high that must not be broken. We don't believe we are free to ignore the law, even if it kills us to obey it. We quite literally accept the notion that the law is what is supreme and the law is what is noble and that it is the law that must be defended at all costs. We give our lives to protect the law. The fact is, that makes no sense. At all.

The law can't be supreme, only our lives can hold supreme meaning. Laws cannot be noble, only people can be noble. The law doesn't need to be defended, because it can't be harmed; in fact, it doesn't even exist except inside people's heads. People need to be defended, because we can be harmed, we can cease to exist. And because we are irreplaceable and life is sacred, we need to take steps to defend and protect life. Therefore, giving our lives to defend something that can't be harmed makes no sense. What is the law for if it is not to protect and defend our lives?

Here are a couple of obvious basics about laws, which will probably not come as any surprise. In the first place, the law and the rules are nothing more than words. They are words written on paper or posted on signs. The words do not come from on high, or from beyond, nor are they eternal and immutable. They are not by any means guaranteed to be fair, or right, or moral, or correct, and there is no legal obligation for them to be any of those things.

Laws are in fact wholly arbitrary and they are written to protect the interests of those who write them. That's why law in its current form exists. That's why it is so heavily propagandized and lauded in countless TV shows where we get all teary-eyed over ideas like justice and righteousness, and we assign only the highest ideals to those who make our laws and those who are heavily armed and will shoot us in the back to uphold them.

Yes, we are trained and taught over and again to obey the laws. We are threatened with frightening stories about what happens when you break the law. We are constantly shown examples of those who break the law. They are held up to us by the scruff of the neck, eyes blackened by police brutality and torture, all legal, of course, and we are told hair-raising stories of their dastardly deeds and the wrongs they've done to the innocent. The message is clear: only bad people break the law. And when the law is broken, terrible things are the consequence. Without the law to steady the keel of social order our whole system would break down and devolve into chaos and disorder, violence and cruelty, and it would all go to shit overnight. It would end everything.

Excuse me while I yawn. Yes, yes, I've heard it all a million times just like you have, but I've actually sat down and thought about it. And what I found out is that, honestly, all of that is pretty much crap. All of it is contrived and designed to keep you and me and everyone else living inside of self-enforced boundaries that prevent us from treading on the lawns of those who want us to believe we have no right to walk wherever we like in a country that we pay for 100 percent. That takes some amazing brainwashing. And we clearly do have that brainwashing, because we all live in utter and desperate fear of doing the wrong thing, or being perceived to have done something wrong, and the mere sight of those glowing red lights in our rear-view mirrors is enough to make even the bravest of us tremble with stomach-churning anxiety.

It's really quite revolting, in my humble opinion. I think it's time for all of us to at least stop long enough to look this whole subject right in the eye and size it up. Let's see what it really is, and who it's all about, and what the reasons and true purposes behind law truly are. This short but interesting adventure could possibly change the way you think of law and rules entirely, and it may very well empower you in ways you never knew existed. It might not do a thing for you, and there are definitely those who will be unable to do this exercise, feeling that they are breaking yet some other unwritten law. The one that says do not question authority. This exercise will indeed separate out those who believe authority is granted by the people from those who believe authority is natural and cast in stone and must never ever be questioned. To those fitting the latter description, you have my condolences. To those who are unafraid to take an intellectual trip into the idea of laws and rules and get a new perspective on things, I say let's do it.

Laws and rules are written by human beings no different than ourselves. The only difference between those who write the laws and make the rules and the rest of us is that they have the pen and they are in the official rooms where our laws are written. That's about it for qualifications. That is it for correctness, righteousness, accuracy, morality, ethics, and every other adjective you might automatically assign to the concept of law. The bottom line is that laws and rules are a man-made thing. They are not necessary to human life. Human life can and has existed and thrived without a single law being in existence. The reality is that life on Earth can get along just fine without man-made laws being imposed on us, we don't need them in any way, shape or form to live a good and meaningful life and do what we're here to do in this world.

It is man-made law that needs us to exist, it cannot continue without us. It needs us to agree to acknowledge it and abide by it, but there is in fact no natural thing, no natural obligation for any humans to obey any man-made laws.

I know that sounds strange, but look at it this way. Think of the other animals in the world, and that is what we are, we are animals, just one of the many kinds of animal life on this planet. Can you name one other animal besides man that obeys any man-made laws? Do dogs and birds and cats keep off the grass because there is a keep off the grass sign posted there? No, they do not. They don't care about any signs, and they don't care about any rules, and it's not just because they can't read. Even if they could read, they still wouldn't care. To them, if a place exists and they want to walk on it, they just go walk on it. The entire concept of permission or allowance or rules would be something they simply would not understand.

To them, the idea of not being allowed to walk somewhere or do anything "because it is against the law" would be meaningless. And that's because it really is meaningless. It's all made up by guys who want things that way, it's not based on any kind of natural law. "NO TRESPASSING" signs will not prevent a single deer or bear or raccoon or rat or cricket or worm from going wherever it wants to. It couldn't care less about any posted signs, and the fact is, it would be very difficult to take aside a raccoon or deer and explain to them that there are laws and that those laws must be obeyed.

The deer, if it could understand you, would listen to you speak, and then it would look at you and say, "Why? Why must I obey any creature on this planet beyond myself? According to who? I am in charge of my life, and this world belongs equally to all who live on it. I need no permission to go anywhere or do anything I like. I may eat whatever I find to eat wherever I find it. The food belongs to no one. If I find it and am eating it, obviously, it is mine to eat. No one else can own it. What a ridiculous idea. You are funny human, and unfortunately not too bright. We animals bow to no man, or beast. We are free, and the world is ours. There are no rulers, rules or laws that are real beyond the laws of nature. We do not recognize your false claims of ownership of what is freely ours and always has been." And they would be right.

There are no other animals than man on the face of the Earth that would give one second's consideration to anyone telling them, "You can't do that!" Animals wouldn't even pause long enough to flip you off. It would literally mean nothing to them what we think or demand of them or each other. Our notions of obligated obedience are complete nonsense to them (and they call *them* the dumb animals).

All the other animals on Earth understand what life is and who they are, and they know the real laws of the world, and they simply live by them. They don't need animal police, and they don't wage animal wars. They don't have animal gangs who run around destroying other animals' homes just for the fun of it or to hoard all of the food even though they could never eat it all but only don't want others to be able to eat. The animals wouldn't put up with that for one second even if it ever did happen in their kingdom.

THE LAW

I'm afraid that whole hoarding and ownership thing is only in our kingdom, and it's no more valid here than it is out there, only we're not smart enough to realize that. Our minds can be gotten into and messed with so much that we no longer understand that we all have the right to food and shelter and life; or at the very least that no one has any conceivable right to prevent us from having those things. Animals know that without needing to talk about it. They have no compulsion to grab it all up for themselves and let all the other animals starve to death or be deprived of the use of the natural shelter all around. It's natural, simple, straightforward, obvious reality.

Animals also don't kill unless it's for food or in self-defense, with the exception of some species' testosterone-saturated males who will sometimes act like jerks and do mean things, but that is the exception, not the norm. Most often these males will fight each other around mating seasons. This is the time that they are driven to prove themselves the strongest, smartest male in the group, and when they achieve that status, the females say, "You will do to father my offspring." It's not very romantic, but it sure is sensible. And the males are happy as can be, because they get to do the one and only thing, more than often, that they're any good for. I'm sorry, but it's true. I don't make this stuff up, check it for yourself.

It is the female, the lioness, who is the hunter and who brings home the bacon for the family. It is the female and the matriarch who is the spiritual leader and boss, from elephants to the humans smart enough to realize that and go with the flow. The males are lazy and aggressive and are often otherwise, sorry, but basically useless and annoying. That's the breaks. That's not to say they aren't a hell of a lot of fun and we'd be lost without them. Okay, I'm having some fun at the expense of males, I couldn't resist. Males are indeed needed, and they are pretty cool.

One example of a very cool male is a 500-pound silverback gorilla. They are so strong they could tear your head off in a second, but you know what? They don't. There's something there worth noticing. The amazing power these creatures have is not something they abuse, even though they could abuse it for personal gain anytime they wanted to. They have no desire to abuse others with their power. Once again, this

143

is an aberration mostly human animals suffer from, with our powerful males feeling no compulsion at all to restrain their ability to abuse others for personal gain or just for the pleasure it gives them to do it. They get off on it. For the gorillas, self-restraint is a natural law that does not require policing to enforce. It only requires being a natural animal to understand the world they live in, and they have a natural respect for the lives of others. Why would they be motivated to be abusive of anyone? What would it get them that they don't already have? You see, it's not a burden for them. It's common sense based on the reality and truth of natural law.

It's really very simple and reasonable when we're talking natural law. It only gets complicated when we're talking about human-made laws, because those are basically a whole lot of crap. The whole point of human-made laws is to prevent people from doing certain things. That's really what it boils down to, and it's not always a bad idea. Sometimes the best thing a community can do is get together and decide things like, it's not okay for people to kill each other just because they want your stuff. It's not okay to walk into someone else's house and take their stuff. It's not okay to hurt people because you want their stuff or just because you don't like them. Everyone agrees to the rules, because they're equal and logical and they apply to everyone in a fair and sensible way.

Having those rules in place makes sense and it allows the people of that community to have a shared value system, which can be a very good thing. It lets people feel safer as they go about their business and it allows steps to be taken when someone breaks the rules and causes harm or damage to others that is unfair or unjustified. It makes their community a nicer place to live, because they've agreed they won't be victimized by evil people and they will stand together and run those bad guys out of town or otherwise deal with them. It's all just too tiresome, frustrating and time consuming when bad guys breeze in and rape and pillage the place every five minutes, and face it, who wouldn't get real tired of that sort of thing? Laws are put in place to define an agreed-upon right and wrong and to uphold and defend that shared agreement to benefit the whole community. It's a good arrangement for a group of honorable people to live by.

THE LAW

The trouble is, mankind is often not very honorable. In fact, some people are downright rotten to the core. They will lie and overstate things, make false claims and accusations, and they do it to get something they don't deserve but want anyway. And they aren't ashamed of it in the least, at least until they get caught and are proven to be greasy slimy liars who end up in jail. That's another series of laws we quickly passed, "No greasy slimy liars when it comes to public dealings." You can do it at home with your own family, but not to anyone else, because we don't have to put up with your private tyranny and delusions of grandeur and entitlement to have it all your way. There is no such thing in the real world, pal, so keep it to yourself. (Unless, of course, you're the President of the United States. He's "the decider," according to him. Like I said, delusions of grandeur.)

It's all quite reasonable. And to the extent that the laws are made and agreed to by the same people who will have to follow them, then it's a pretty good deal. They can change their laws when they need changing, and no one is forced to comply with anything against their will.

But the laws have to be fair and treat everyone equal or it's not law anymore, it's corruption. And all of that is easy to see when you're directly involved in your own self-governing. Where the people *are* the law, it's quite difficult for a cadre of weasels to move in and take over, because they have no power over anyone else.

And that's precisely why the entire idea of power over others was shoved into the law books. Human weasels exist. They are real and they want to be in charge of others. If you think about it for a minute, it should become apparent why anyone would want to have power over others. Claiming that you have power over others entitles you to get away with wrongdoing. It entitles you to treat others unfairly and prevent them from being able to do anything to protect themselves from you. Power over others is great for the sociopaths who crave it so badly. Power over others is not a normal thing to want, and most of us would have little desire for it.

Power over others is not a natural thing. It is not necessary and it is rarely something people welcome. We don't like anyone having power over our lives, and we don't need it. It doesn't help us in any way. When anyone has power over our lives, it only helps them, those who have the power. It enables them to decide what the rules are, regardless of whether we like it or not, and there are only two rules once power over others is introduced into the law books:

- RULE NUMBER ONE is that he who has the guns makes the rules.
- RULE NUMBER TWO is that he who has the money makes the rest of the rules.

There is no rule number three. That's all of it. It doesn't matter if there are a million laws on the books, those are the two that it all boils down to. And they say the law is too complicated to understand. Nope. It's as simple as can be.

Those who are represented by rule number one, and those who are represented by rule number two may disagree with the ranking order, but that's really nothing that affects the rest of us. It doesn't matter who's number one, the end result is all the same to those who don't get to make any of the rules. What it boils down to for us is that the rich people will make rules all day and all night that say rich people matter and you don't, and the guys with the guns will show up and get you if you don't happen to like those rules. That's our whole legal system in a nutshell. Go ahead and tell me I'm wrong. You can't. That really is what it is. Something else it is, is totally invalid.

The laws that put power over others on the books are false laws based on nothing valid. Power over others is not a necessity of life. We don't need no stinkin' power over others, nor do we need anyone to have power over us. We would do just fine, thank you, without power on this Earth. We'd be fine, we would thrive, we would get along somehow without being told what we cannot do by twits who think they own us. It is they who would not fare well. They would cease to be. It is they who need us in order to continue existing, not the other way around. That is what I mean when I say "natural" law.

Because what is the law really if it is not the law of life? If it is not the law of simple truth? If our man-made laws are not the written expression of human truth, then they can't be valid. And the fact is, we don't need laws to be written if they are natural laws, because natural laws can't be broken. Natural laws cannot be shot dead or eradicated or destroyed or corrupted. They just are what they are, because that's what they are.

For instance, it is a natural law that females give birth. You can pass a man-made law that requires men to give birth, and women will be arrested if they keep it up, but you already know that man-made law won't change a thing. It's a stupid law. It's demanding that natural law be subordinated to some stupid human's idiotic will. It doesn't work that way and there's nothing you can do about it.

As amusing as that may be, it is not a silly measurement of validity, it's really quite valid, and it's something more serious and real and worthy of our consideration than those men who make our millions of man-made laws would like us to notice.

There really is such a thing as natural justice. We are all capable of knowing what feels fair and right. We are capable of witnessing acts and of knowing right away if they were just and fair or criminally unjust. It's a simple thing to determine, and this again is something we need no man-made laws to frame or define for us.

Justice is within us, and it is self-evident; when we know the given facts, we can come up with the just conclusions. It's a beautiful thing that the rest of the animal world enjoys every day. But in our part of the animal kingdom we can't seem to get everyone to play fair and be honest, or be reasonable, or be led by a sense of justice or fairness. In the human animal, there is an anomaly, people who don't care about what's fair or right or just and who have no interest in anything beyond getting what they want for themselves no matter who it belongs to or who they must hurt or cheat to get it. These people are obviously not right in the head, but unfortunately, these people tend to be the ones that make our laws, because they are also the ones who crave all that power over everyone. It is because of them that our whole system of laws has turned into the convoluted polluted mess of incomprehensible legalese spaghetti it is today.

Our laws are now too many and too confusing to be of any use to the vast majority of us. We literally need to hire consultants who spend their entire lives buried in law books to have any chance of making our way through the nightmare that is our legal system. This system is not user friendly, and it doesn't even try to be.

The law has become so far removed from the average citizen that it has become a monster. It consumes us in our ignorance. Because the law and those who "uphold" it are both self-concerned and self-worshiping, there is little doubt that our current system of so-called law and order, our system of justice, is only concerned with it's own power and continued control over the public and very little else.

We are always right to challenge the law anytime we see it working in contradiction to simple truth and justice, and sadly, it often does just that. The bottom line is that our system of laws is no more real or valid or powerful than we decide to let it be, and although it would claim to have power over us, it does not and cannot, there is no mechanism or proof of any such thing. We can walk away from it any time we like and just blow it off. We can say, "You are invalid and we are no longer interested in playing your stupid power games that control us and our lives and are patently unfair. Leave us alone, you are nothing. We are better off without you." We can indeed turn and walk away anytime, and that is the truth, the natural law, our birthright, something that cannot be changed. It is the reality of human law. It is always up to us what our own laws are, and it is always up to us whether or not to accept them, obey them, abide by them or have anything to do with them. The only power human law has is the power we give it. And the power we give it can also be taken away, by us.

That is the reality of power, and the fact is that reality has been subverted and propagandized by very clever, very devious, very evil people who have sold us the notion that they must have power over us to keep us safe. That is always a lie. No one can keep us safe. If you think that through, you'll realize the truth of it.

Fear is the tool that enslaves us. And nonexistent power is what keeps us beneath those who feed off of us and deprive us of natural justice.

There are no beings on this planet who have any entitlement to control others. In order to do so they must use force, and that is never legitimate power, obviously. Force is not power, it is force. It is the lowest form of human existence on this planet. Any moron can be violent, it takes no thought or intellect or talent. Force is the cheap trick that seeks to cover the truth of its own invalidity with the blood of others. It is never respected, it is never valid, and it is what lies at the core of the laws that we are forced to endure and live by today.

That threat of force is with us at all times, and it is never concerned with justice. It is only concerned with our total compliance. It is instantly exerted at the slightest sign of our disobedience or disagreement. I would say that the legitimacy of our entire system of laws is in serious question, because when laws are just, there is no need to use force against anyone. Why the need for such brutality, if this is such a just system of laws? Why the lust for such extreme punishment, if this system is so fair, reasonable and compassionate?

People everywhere are all too happy to live in a just world, and many of us would really like to try it. It is usually only when people are deprived of justice that they refuse to comply with the laws, and when they do that, they are severely punished. Who does it serve to condition us to see government brutality and murder of citizens for failure to obey the law as a valid thing for governments to do? It doesn't serve us. It serves them. We are never threatened by the public airing of grievances to determine what is fair and what is right. Only the governments of the world are threatened by the idea of real justice for the people. Are you beginning to see the pattern?

This is the ugly reality, and the truth is that power corrupts. The entire notion of power is something to reconsider, because as far as I can tell, it really has no validity in this world.

Our American freedom is a grand illusion, and the law is only a tool of those who want to control us so badly. It is the highest trick they have, which they alone can use to get us to believe they have such a thing as power over our lives. This is why they do their business in court.

If we rejected this unnatural man-made system of law, what device would exist that they could use to convince us that we are obligated to do things their way? What device could they point to and claim that by virtue of this device they have control and power over all of our lives? There is no such device. Nothing exists that allows others' power and control over us except this one thing: not the law itself, for it has no power or virtue on its own, but only our belief that the law must never be broken. That belief alone is what perpetuates the status quo and allows this broken system to continue with no hope of our cleaning it up and making it honest. We don't have the power to do that. We only have the power to walk away, but they have ways of dealing with that too. They seem pretty desperate, don't they, if that's what it takes to keep people under their control. There is nothing about their claims to power and control that is valid enough to make it unnecessary for them to use force against us, to force our compliance with their laws and self-interested demands.

This is also why they control the courts, and why the courts and all who work in them work for those who control us and claim to have power over our lives. The courts do not exist for us and they do not exist to bring justice. They exist as a tool of officialdom and majik to make us believe that when we are deprived of justice in court that they have won fair and square and we are obliged to accept whatever they say. It is a tool that enables them to retain false power and control regardless of truth or justice.

It's all quite obvious once you see it, it's right there for all to see. If we can see through the propaganda that makes us all believe that just because it is a law it must be respected and obeyed and upheld, we could set ourselves free from our self-imposed self-limiting erroneous beliefs. That we must obey all laws and rules is nothing but a huge propaganda job that's done on our minds, not for our benefit, but for theirs. If those who control us were truly interested in justice, it would be they who would be explaining this to you, not me. But they will never be this honest, because the risk is just too high that we would reject their phony power and reject their control and deny their false claims to run the world to their liking. If it was our choice, we would choose natural justice to rule ourselves, and we would make them go away. And they know that.

And now you know it too. Interesting, yes? Do you look at the law any different now? Geez, I hope so. And I hope it's gotten you closer to the reality that we're all consistently denied knowledge of. The power really does belong to us, and we can change it all any time we like. The constitution doesn't give us the right to live in a just world, natural law gives us that right. That is the real natural law that can never be broken. It belongs to us all, and it always will. If only we knew it, maybe we could finally put an end to the injustice that rules our world and begin the simple work it would take to make our world a better place for everyone.

Wednesday, May 14, 2008.

On Being Fully Here

In a beautiful remote corner of the world there is a vast and deep gorge separating this side from that side. A grand old oak tree swirled in a coat of wet fog stands at the nearest edge. As you approach, you breathe in deeply. The air is fresh and electric and the sound of a rushing river below rebounds off patches of thick, clinging fog. You've come to the edge.

Just like I told you, it is there. A great rope bridge that spans the width of the canyon. It is strong and secure, very well made. It seems magical hanging there. How did humans make this and manage to get it across this vast separation of land masses?

You are not afraid as you step onto the rope bridge and place your hand on the edge to guide you. You begin to walk. You came a long way to get here. It's a moment you've been waiting for all your life. As you walk through the fog, your footsteps gently echo off the rock walls of the gorge. The mist of a waterfall brushes against your cheek. Just keep walking. While you walk, I'll talk. I want to tell you something.

This may sound odd, but it's still true. I have never fully been here, on Earth, until now. I've been here physically. I've been here mentally. But an entire huge, fundamental and most important part of me has not been here.

All my life I sensed this, but could not know it, and no one I could have asked, if there was a way to ask, would have known what I was talking about. Because by and large the people who comprised my life experience before now did not have this part of their being with them either. Their experience was exactly the same as mine, not in the physical details, but due to unrecognized yet inescapable applied methods and their inevitable results. I think this applies to most everyone, and I also think that very few people are ever allowed to be fully here, much to our personal detriment, and definitely to the general serious detriment of planet Earth.

We hear of the soul, of the mind, of consciousness and higher self. There are all kinds of words that mean all kinds of things that just don't explain anything very well. What do they mean when they say "soul"? The word "mind" is so dry and generalized, what does it mean? What about extrasensory perception? Precognition? Knowing when someone is lying or telling the truth? The spectrum of emotions that accompany every moment of our lives, where does that come from?

Because all these words tend to confuse more than clarify, I use the term "invisible self" and allow that to mean the whole of my being that is not strictly physical and measurable. Because truly it is everything beyond that which is physical and measurable, that is who we are. That is where the rubber hits the road, so to speak. That people have physical bodies and limbs and that we can observe that people are conscious, can do math, can memorize things and learn how to spell and read, says literally nothing about who they are. Not a single thing.

I am much more than that stuff, and everyone I know is more than that. But the sad fact is that we are given to believe that who we are stops there, at physical form and education levels, and that whatever else there is beyond that is mostly superfluous. But it's not superfluous, it's the whole point I exist. Everything beyond that stuff is who I really am. It is me.

This is the part that is castrated by the demands of social conformity; the part that is rejected by authority and doctrine and those who would be our gods on Earth. And there's a reason for that. It's the part that threatens every established thing in the world. It could threaten every established authority, every rule and law, every social standard, and every perspective on life and the way things are in this world. This is the part where the most important and meaningful work happens in the course of an individual human being's life. It's the only place, the only part of our being where we can evolve.

This part of our invisible self is where we are creative and noble and wise. Where all facets of our being can be unleashed free of influence from others. It's like a grand private workroom where everything we know and learn and experience is stored, and we can go in there and put all these pieces together, in our own way, without anyone else butting in or being involved or being able to control us. This is where we apply imagination to what is already known to see new things and see old things in new ways. It's where we can explore the entirety of who we are and do the ongoing work of creating ourselves; and in so doing we can and will bring new influences to the world.

I've come not just to believe this, but to know it as fact, that there are entities, forces, people, call them whatever you like, who don't want mankind to know about this denied part of ourselves. It totally threatens the stranglehold these forces have on the world in literally almost every detail. They are working tirelessly around the clock too, with unlimited funding, recruiting the finest scientific minds to figure out how to make sure that humanity is once and for all cut off from that part of themselves. Only in so doing can these interests be certain that they will not be challenged and revealed for who and what they are.

Only if people are taught to disregard any notions of there being more than what can be measured and tested can people be led away from fully existing. If people are taught to laugh at and put down as idiotic anyone's assertions that things exist beyond what we can see, then people can be led away from being fully human and fully existing in their one short lifetime. We are told there's nothing out there, there is nothing more to our minds or beings, when the reality is that there is everything beyond those falsely asserted cut off points. Everything we are and ever can be lies beyond those fake imposed boundaries.

Getting past those boundaries is the furthest thing away from mysterious and spooky, it requires no special skills or teaching. Every child is born easily and joyously existing in their full being. The job of greater society is to coax every one of us out of our creative centers, out of the grand workrooms of self and life and all that matters most, and to shut the door behind us, and pull the drapes across it, and to never mention it again.

That part of self is not gone. It is abandoned and unused, it may be atrophied and dormant. But because it is a living thing, a part of the invisible self, it can be resuscitated and rejuvenated. The windows can be thrown open to let the sunshine in, and it can very much feel like home. It can hurt, because it means we must at times reject what everyone else believes and go against the grain. This often causes tension, and worse, and that has to be less important to us than taking full possession of our true and full potential. What "everyone believes" is often wrong and is the major roadblock between us and ourselves, and if we really want to get there, we have to remove the roadblock.

I said it was hard, but as far as I'm concerned, it's so worth it, it's not even funny. I feel anger and resentment that it took so long for me to find this out, and I had to do it myself, and it was the hardest work I've ever done. But the pay-offs have been more than I ever knew were possible. Not doing this would have been to waste my entire life, and what a terrible, painful shame that would have been. One has to fully be here to exist, or you're just showing up in a shell, a costume, and playing a role on a stage for someone else's benefit. We might as well be made of cardboard and stood up in a corner for all that's worth in the course of a lifetime.

Our disconnection from the whole of ourselves is something we're all perfectly aware of. It's that restlessness inside that never goes away, even when we have what we want and need. It's that empty hole that's like a hunger for more, for meaning, for something else, for substance, and it can't be filled by buying something or by taking drugs or drinking or sleeping around or extreme bowling or being a fanatic starstruck follower of fashion. No external label we try to apply to define ourselves will fill that hole, because that hole cannot be filled by anything outside of ourselves. The fact that you feel the hunger, the emptiness, the need for something else exposes a truth. Allowing yourself to reopen that closed down part of your invisible self will be the challenge and reward that will feed you again and again. It's not a one-time thing, nothing about staying alive is a one-time thing. This, like every part of yourself, is something you incorporate seamlessly and use every day of your life. It's not separate from you, it is you.

What's missing from your life is you. A part of you that you've been told can't exist, but there it is anyway. It's you. An unused, unrecognized and truly not wanted by external forces major part of you. The real you. It's not a secret or a sin or anything to apologize for, it's you.

I do believe that people will stop searching externally and in vain for all of their answers once they realize how much of their search is for that lost and buried part of themselves. There are external answers to be sure, but if there are external answers, then there must also be internal ones. We do become conditioned to think in terms of there being nothing more of ourselves, that any more is undesirable or problematic, that we have no intrinsic value or creativity or power beyond our physical possessions, and that only certain specific others and types of others who are officially condoned and certified have all the answers and all the importance. It's a total crock.

Why are we so strongly encouraged and pushed to only believe others and go to others for every answer and direction? It makes us neurotic and insecure, obsessive and depressed. It doesn't work. If it did, this should be the healthiest, strongest, most thriving society on the face of the Earth. It's not. It's coming apart at the seams and that's in direct measure to how much experts have taken over our minds and how much conformity and "political correctness" has come to dominate the society. These are tools to shut down original sources, to vilify unique thinking, to frame both personal and natural social evolution as dangerous negatives.

Yet, the more we are required to conform, the sicker and weaker we become. Clearly something is not right. Something is missing. Something we're being told isn't true. We will never get everything we truly need from out there. All we'll get is a pathetic one-size-fits-all crutch for our crippled selves that will make our existence feel stunted to pointless. We are doing it wrong. It is supposed to be much better than this, and we all know it. It can be and it is when we reclaim our mental real estate and begin to figure out the world and ourselves for ourselves.

We need our own culture, we need many diverse cultures, the more the better. We must make our own music and sing songs together instead of buying songs and never singing. We must dance instead of watching experts dance. We don't need to care about doing it right, we need to care about doing it even if we're not experts at it. Who cares about experts? What good do experts really do us? Good for experts, but we've got our own thing, and theirs isn't a part of our personal lives. We need to live life ourselves.

It's quality, not quantity. It's participation, not perfection. It's experiencing, not hoarding. It's caring, not turning our backs. It's having time, not rushing. It's having enough, not too much and not too little. It's about connecting, not separating. Kindness, not cruelty. Courtesy, not rudeness. We count. We all matter. Diversity draws us closer, it does not break us apart. There is no such thing as only one right way. We should be able to see that by now. We should also know that any imposed "one world order" will surely kill us all.

What is all this one world order stuff anyway? This already is one world. What are they babbling about when they say that? It makes no sense. What are they trying to pull? It's a word game, a trick of mind. This has always and only been one world. It's already unified. We already get along. We already have trade and spiritual beliefs and dance and food. What seems to be screwing it up is what power imposes on us, what power demands and inserts and insists upon. Money and power monopoly is the dark interference, the war, the terror and economic blight. I don't think we need no stinking one world order. In fact, I'm sure we don't. It's the last thing we would ever want, because it will demand complete and total conformity, the diminishment of all diversity. One world dogma insists that we decrease ourselves and each other, reduce our minds and bodies, become irrelevant and unimportant. In a great sea of conformity no one stands out. Who wants to live in a world like that?

External forces have outlined and ushered in somebody else's version of what life on Earth is "supposed to be." It's one thing to offer and suggest new things, but it's a whole 'nother thing to force them down our throats at gunpoint, especially with so much underhanded lying and subterfuge. Their ideas are not explained, but hidden. Their purposes are veiled. Secrecy is becoming the norm of power, money and corruption are inseparable, and violence and force have replaced justice. We are being led to a cage where we will be forced to comply or die. Their ideas are crap. We don't need them or want them.

The idea of success itself is an external one, and the definition of success is completely externally-created and imposed. That doesn't make it right or real or all that desirable. The definition of education is wholly made up by others and imposed. How much of what you think of yourself is based on someone else's imposed definitions? No one has the legitimacy to define anything for anyone else, that's square one and people have always known that much. It's taken many years and much underground effort and cash to slowly convince the world that we should all follow and only official others should be the leaders. They are selling us bullshit. It doesn't stand up when looked in the eye. It's all crap. Today, all officialdom is crap.

We're not to think this way, at least that is the message every single one of us has somehow managed to have deeply implanted within us. We think it wrong and naughty to have our own opinions and we'd never boldly speak them in defiance of set standards of thought and opinion. At least a lot of people don't. And they don't, because somewhere deep inside we have actually accepted the false assertion, the strange notion that someone else's so-called expert or official opinion has more validity than our own. That speaks to how little we think of ourselves and how subjugated and servile we have slowly become, to the point that by and large this society is mentally pathetic and shut off and stuck in rote circular movements that take us nowhere. Except to work each day, and then we die. By listening to and believing only outside sources we are learning to cease to exist. That's a big red flag, as I see it.

I would say there is more to life than what we're given and expected and pressured to believe. A hell of a lot more. I think it's time we flung open those doors within our minds, the doors that so many others have forced shut and locked and covered with curtains until we forget those doors are there. I say, rip away those dusty old drapes and toss them out of your head. Open that door and walk right on through. You get to be, to become, you get to be who you are, why wouldn't you? Who says you shouldn't or can't? Who are they to say such stupid things? Our masters? Our owners? Our bosses? I don't think so. I know nobody's my master, no human being can be more than my equal. I won't live on my knees to anyone, why should I? Why should you? Why should anyone be expected to? What nonsense.

It's no wonder that our self-esteem is so damaged in this society, it is devastating to have the bulk of ourselves and what really matters forcibly closed down as we grow up. All we get are messages of conformity and the expectation to conform. We are rewarded and approved of when we conform, and when we're super-conformers, we get a gold star. This is true in kindergarten, and it stays true throughout any professional career. Conformist thinkers, conformist workers, supporters of the powers that be, those who excuse the obvious inequities and flaws and abject failures and crimes of the status quo, who are blind to being used and used up by those in control of our lives, they are patted on the head and told "good girl" and "good boy." The rewards don't go much beyond that. It just goes to show how desperate we become for approval and notice, when who we are is defined by outside sources instead of the only source that really matters.

Nothing comes without a downside, though, and there's no exception here. We don't get through life alone. We need others. We very much need good guidance, we need to be taught many important things, and we, unfortunately or fortunately as the case may be, usually don't have any choice about who those teachers are or what they teach. Good parents teach us right from wrong, not under threat, but by explaining why. They teach us how to think past the obvious, think for ourselves, and encourage us to be independent, while at the same time achieve a balance that allows us to work and live and be with others and respect them.

It takes skill and conscious work to become a decent human being. And that's why I say I haven't really been here, even though I seemed to be. I didn't know that there was more than achieving conformity or that I wouldn't begin to exist until I shrugged off that erroneous belief and got to work on finding out who I am and what life is about for myself. No one ever said as much or explained the fact that it was a life-long, ongoing job, and a hard one, to make myself into who I am and who I want to be. Someone I am not ashamed of or embarrassed about, not based on external standards, which are meaningless, but based on my own values and beliefs. Beliefs that aren't just handed to me and absorbed without thought, but which I pull apart and explore and test until I get it and see the value in them and own them myself. It would have been nice to get the heads up on this before so much of my life had gone by.

That is the insidious nature of believing without questioning, and it is all but impossible to refuse to conform when everyone around you is a true believer in conformity. Even when you can see that none of them have ever thought it through, that they've simply taken on as their own what someone else devised not for the greater good of society, but to enrich themselves at everyone else's cost, very few will stop to hear you out. But better late than never at all. It's great to find out that there is always room for self-correction and improvement, and that's a good thing, not evidence of being flawed, and that it's never too late, too much to ask, or unnecessary to face yourself and fix what's in the way of being a real person. We're not perfect, but we are always capable of self-repair and growth and even great change, if we desire it. It is the hardest work we can ever do, but it's work worth doing. At least that's what I've come to see. Without doing the hard work of really finding out what we're made of and who we really are, we can be no more than what our external generic society demands of us, and that's just not enough for me. I realize it is more than enough for some people, and I have to say I feel sorry for those people. But it's not my call what they choose for themselves. If being what others dictate makes them happy, then who am I to criticize? But I doubt very much they are happy. I doubt very much their deepest inner hunger is ever fed.

This is why people search for answers, knocking on the doors of every religious establishment and spiritual theory hoping to find a resonance that feels like self. But, of course, it's nowhere out there, it's inside them. When they have that, then they can likely go to any religion or spiritual school and benefit from it, but likely not before and not without. They'd only forever have questions, and not really understand the teachings. Someone would always be their master, when they are supposed to be their own master. These are my beliefs, not facts, I can't prove them. I observe these things, and I have questions about it all, and I spend lots of time in my own workroom hammering out answers, fitting the pieces together and coming back out with a section that fits in here, and one that fits in there, as I slowly grow the overall picture to completion. Or at least the first picture. There are likely many more.

There is so much loneliness, anguish and resentment out there; and violence and depravity are springing up like weeds in the absence of real people growing real selves. People have been lied to and confused, and now they think that sex is love and are confounded when they find out it isn't, because it's supposed to be. There's nothing else out there, the external sources assert through pictures and movies and pornography and books, that's supposed to do it. You need "good looks," and six-pack abs, and a nice car, and you have to work out and have your hair cut just so, and wear the right clothes, and have the right job, and feel sexually attracted to someone, and that's supposed to do it. But none of that has a thing to do with love.

It's no big shock that this society is busted apart and lonely, separated and silent, afraid and starving with no end in sight. Love is a place, not a thing, and true beauty comes after love, not before, but we aren't told about any of that. We aren't told the truth about anything, in fact. I fear for the future of mankind. I fear that it won't be long before our inner starvation allows us to accept being modified and chipped and augmented until there is no more humanity. Until we are all products that perform functions and don't care about love, or meaning, or that part of ourselves that won't just be hidden, but will finally be forever gone.

Should man create other men? Should mankind take it upon himself to make other men into his own image? Or shouldn't each person make himself into a better person, his own way, with his own mind? We have yet to reach our full potential as human beings, and external augmentation is not the means to get there, that is only the final detour. That is the final path away from being everything we can be as human beings. What a shame that someone out there, some group of very strange people, have such a strong driving need to destroy mankind, to undermine humanity, to enslave it and humiliate it, and teach us all to believe that we have no value and we don't matter and we can't think for ourselves or be more than we are. I don't know what would possess these powerful people to so despise the world, but they do. And we are endangered to the literal edge of our extinction. The wars and genocides are all a part of some grotesque greater plan, and separating the human being from himself is the beginning and end of hope for our species.

In case it needs to be said, we don't have to go along with anything that we know is evil or wrong or destructive. We do not ever have to choose to be devalued and disrespected by anyone who claims to be more important than ourselves. They can only be more important if we choose to believe they are and thus deny and subjugate ourselves. But it must be asked, why would we do that? When anyone says that we must be less than we are because they say so, we already know they're lying. We already know that no legitimate being would tell us to be less than we are so they can be happy. That's not love. That's not respect. It's not even reasonable. It's the overt demand that we stop existing. That's slow death from the inside out. On a vast scale, when all of society gets down on its knees to mere men who say they must, it is spiritual genocide. We are free to stop doing it anytime.

No part of ourselves can be taken from us by someone else, it can only be destroyed or undermined. No one else can reduce us, we can only reduce ourselves when we believe the exquisite lies we are told. Perhaps a simple rule of thumb that might expose those who claim to be our betters is to notice if what they ask of us makes us less or more than we already are. If it makes us less, then it is a part of the incremental destruction of mankind. Little by little, bit by bit, it's hardly painful, at least not right away. But cumulatively over decades humanity is changed, reduced, lessened, weakened, lost, dependent, and finally ceases to exist.

We are up against something so evil that it's hard to believe it could exist. But it does. We have only to look around us to see that it exists. I don't know why, and I don't know much else about it, but I can see that much with the naked eye. I feel the outrage they evoke with their endless insults against my kind, humanity, with their endless removal of justice and fairness, with their disrespect and lies, and their endless assertions that money is king and all-important and the measure of a man.

They are sheer evil, and we are up shit creek if we don't wake up and tell them where to shove it. We must create ourselves. We have to know the difference between real teachers and real leaders and fake ones. The ones who make life better and bring us more are the real deal. The ones who don't should be rejected, shamed and exposed.

By the way, that rope bridge you're walking on, that's your bridge, and you should have guessed by now where it goes. What's on the other side is the rest of you, and nobody gets to say you can't go there. Of course, you can. The real complaint is that those who want you to cease to exist, they can't go there. Thank God for that.

It is always and only your choice to keep walking or turn back and blend in with the rest of conforming society. You will always be rewarded for conforming. It's a guaranteed paycheck, albeit a wholly inadequate one. I would not be able to resist exploring what I found in my own private world. I couldn't bear never knowing who or what I could be, what I'm made of, how I really think and feel about things. I see every single thing I thought I knew completely differently now. All I had to add to the mix was my whole being. It is my sincere wish that everyone would cross their own bridge and find the most amazing and wonderful part of themselves, and own it and enjoy it and live life empowered and strengthened by it. Everything there is, is over there to discover. It's a very interesting place to be.

Be advised that bridge is the most hated enemy of those who would be Earth's new rulers. They're cutting away the ropes, you know, chewing through the fibers one by one. Bit by bit lengths of rope are falling off, down into the water below. There will come a time, when you no longer have the option of crossing your own bridge. They don't want you to have that option. They don't want you to go over there. They don't want you to know yourself or any other truth about anything. They don't want you asking your own questions and providing your own answers. They don't want any of us to get it into our heads that they are not our owners. They want us to sit down and shut up and do as we are told.

ON BEING FULLY HERE

If that works for you, then you'll be fine. Don't do a thing, it's coming. If it doesn't work for you, you might want to keep on walking. If you do keep on walking, after you get there and after a while, when you're settled in and feel quite at home, would you do something for me? Drop me a postcard. I love getting postcards.

Tuesday, February 17, 2009.

Printed in Great Britain
by Amazon